WITHDRAWN

JUSTINIAN II
OF
BYZANTIUM

JUSTINIAN II
OF
BYZANTIUM

Constance Head

THE UNIVERSITY OF WISCONSIN PRESS
Madison, Milwaukee, and London

(Inventory 1977)

Published 1972
The University of Wisconsin Press
Box 1379, Madison, Wisconsin 53701

The University of Wisconsin Press, Ltd.
70 Great Russell Street, London, WC1B 3BY

FIRST PRINTING

Printed in the United States of America
NAPCO, Inc., Milwaukee, Wisconsin

ISBN 0-299-06030-6; LC 79-161497

CONTENTS

ILLUSTRATIONS

MAPS

PREFACE

THERE are few sovereigns in Byzantine history more interesting than Justinian II, the emperor who lost his nose but who never lost his will to rule, who lived for ten years in exile, wandered among the barbarians, escaped innumerable dangers, and finally regained his throne only to lose it again. Yet, if he is among the most colorful of the emperors, Justinian II is also among the most obscure. The period in which he lived—the late seventh and the early eighth century—is an epoch unusually poor in source material. It was a crucial era, a time when great events were taking place in East and West, yet because so few sources have survived, it remains an era neglected by historians. Thus while a great deal is known about the earlier development of the Byzantine (or East Roman) Empire, the relative lack of first-hand sources has rendered the seventh and eighth centuries a veritable Byzantine Dark Age. Many volumes have been written about the justly famous sixth-century emperor Justinian I, yet there has never been a book-length study of Justinian II. Moreover, in many of the larger works where the second Justinian's reign is accorded some treatment, historians have tended to accept data from the meager early chronicle sources in a rather uncritical manner.

Still, in spite of the difficulties of research in this obscure period, the very neglect which it has been accorded points to the need for further scholarly effort. The present volume by no means claims to be a definitive study of Justinian II; it is designed more for the student of history and the general reader than for the specialist. Byzantine scholars will notice at once that the primary materials used have long been known; there is nothing really new here in the way of source information. Nevertheless, readers who possess an extensive background in Byzantine history will recognize, too, that this presentation of Justinian II's history at times departs considerably from the usual interpretation of his actions.

I first became interested in Justinian because of the intrinsic fascination of his life story, yet I believed at the outset of my research that he was completely as the early chroniclers picture him: irresponsible, intensely cruel, devoid of any redeeming features. Then, during the course of my studies, I became increasingly impressed by numerous small bits and pieces of evidence revealing Justinian as an intelligent statesman and a conscientious sovereign. It became clear, also, that apparently no effort had been made to collect these items into one work and thereby to muster a formidable challenge to the adverse evaluation that has come down to us from the early chronicles. Particularly is this true of his second reign. Historians who have dealt with this period have often become so preoccupied with the chroniclers' gruesome tales of the disfigured emperor, driven by frantic desire for vengeance, that they have made no real attempt to consider in a more balanced light what Justinian was trying to do.

Justinian II, Emperor of the Byzantines, lived in a violent and troubled era, and undoubtedly there was in his character a reflection of the violence of the age in which he lived. It would be as serious an error to discard the chroniclers' reports entirely as it is to accept their every word as historical fact. Justinian made many grave mistakes, especially in his second reign, mistakes which a man of more balanced judgment and calmer temperament would have avoided.

Still, above all, it is to be remembered that this emperor of thirteen centuries ago was a human being: living, working, planning, worrying, as people generally do. He was, moreover, a man who bore great tragedy and who eventually had to learn to live with the inescapable reality of his disfigurement. For all these reasons, he invites our understanding. To contribute to such understanding is the major objective of this work, and it is my hope that from it will emerge a clearer picture of Justinian II of Byzantium, both as a sovereign and as a person.

CONSTANCE HEAD

Cullowhee, North Carolina
July 1971

Acknowledgments

I wish to express gratitude to all the following individuals and institutions who have assisted in various ways in the completion of this book:

To the editors of *Byzantion* for permission to incorporate parts of my article "Towards a Reinterpretation of the Second Reign of Justinian II" (*Byzantion* 40 [1970]: 14–32) in this work.

To Dumbarton Oaks Center for Byzantine Studies for permission to reproduce photos of coins from the Dumbarton Oaks Collection.

To the personnel of the Cartographic Laboratory of the University of Wisconsin, who produced the maps.

To Professor John W. Barker of the University of Wisconsin, who read the manuscript and made many helpful suggestions.

To Professors Charles R. Young, Ray C. Petry, and W. F. Stinespring of Duke University and Max R. Williams of Western Carolina University, all of whom read parts of the manuscript at earlier stages and gave me the benefit of their constructive criticism.

To Mr. Emerson Ford of Duke University and Mrs. Joan K. Leseuer of Western Carolina University for obtaining much-needed and often-hard-to-find materials through Interlibrary Loan.

And most of all to my mother, who first taught me to love history and who has been the source of unfailing encouragement through my five years' research on Justinian II.

JUSTINIAN II
OF
BYZANTIUM

1

JUSTINIAN'S WORLD

CONSTANTINE IV, Emperor of Byzantium, was a blond, handsome youth of seventeen when his eldest son Justinian was born in the Year of Our Lord 669. *Justinian*: the name itself was heavy with significance. More than a hundred years earlier (527–565) the magnificent Justinian the Great, lawgiver and builder extraordinary, had ruled the Byzantine world, and the fame of his achievements had never been forgotten. To the young emperor Constantine this splendid predecessor was the embodiment of the imperial ideal, the model whom he longed to emulate. Thus, although he could claim no blood relationship with his hero, he departed from the custom of his own dynasty in which the eldest son was always called Constantine or Heraclius and bestowed upon his first-born the glorious name of Justinian. It was a heritage which, for good or ill, would influence Justinian II all his life: he was to grow up intensely proud of his name and of the great emperor who had borne it before him, so much, in fact, that at times he consciously attempted to imitate the exploits of Justinian I.

Ironically, however, history would not accord to the second Justinian the enduring fame that even to this day surrounds the reputation of the first one. With the passing of centuries, he has become so generally forgotten that historians rarely even bother to attach the imperial number "I" to his namesake, tacitly implying by its omission that no other

Emperor Justinian ever existed. Justinian II, we may be sure, would be most unhappy over this historiographical quirk.

But in spite of the undue neglect with which history has treated him, diligent searching reveals a surprising amount of information about this highly unconventional sovereign. The events of his life story—the cruel disfigurement of his face and loss of his throne, his years of exile and his wanderings among tribes beyond the frontiers of his empire, the heroism of the barbarian girl who loved him and whom he made his empress when he had regained his throne, his eventual death at the hands of a mutinous army—comprise a narrative stranger than fiction. Moreover, through the all-too-meager sources relating these adventures, the character of the man himself is always close to the surface: Justinian of Byzantium, born to the purple, imperious, hot-tempered, willful, sometimes cruel, yet indisputably brave and intelligent and above all possessed of invincible determination to overcome adversity. He is, in brief, a man still very much alive across a gulf of thirteen centuries.

Justinian is more, however, than a fascinating personality; for sixteen years (685–695 and 705–711) he was head of state of the strongest Christian nation in the world of his time, and as such would have vast impact upon the development of his empire at one of the most crucial eras in its long history.

What sort of state was this Byzantine Empire in the early medieval centuries? All too often historians have tended to picture it merely as a curious afterglow of imperial Rome. It is true that to the Byzantine mind, Constantinople, the imperial capital, was the New Rome; the emperors who reigned there were the successors of the Caesars. But to understand Byzantium as the continuator of the Roman Empire is to see only one aspect of its multifaceted character. Actually Byzantine civilization was a composite of Roman, Greek, oriental, and early Christian ways of thought, blending to produce a culture as distinct from its classical antecedents as it was from the medieval West.

By the seventh century, the Greek title *Basileus* had come to replace the Latin *Augustus* as the favorite title of the

Byzantine emperor—one small indication of the growing preponderance of the Greek heritage over the Roman as medieval Byzantium evolved. To the ancient Greeks, too, can largely be ascribed the love of learning and respect for beautiful things that is so much a part of the Byzantine nature. It was the Byzantines, incidentally, who preserved down through medieval times almost all that we have left of ancient Greek literature and history. And if they are justly to be pronounced not so creative as their Greek forebears in the area of literary achievement, the Byzantines certainly possessed a full measure of originality in the realm of art. Their incomparable mosaics and their magnificent achievements in the construction of domes are but their two best-known contributions in the artistic field. Like much else in the Byzantine world, their art testifies to this people's blending of Near Eastern ideas with the Graeco-Roman heritage to form something unique.

It is the presence of the Near Eastern element that perhaps contributes most to the Byzantine imperial mystique—and to Western difficulty in understanding this long-vanished empire. Oriental ideas of absolute rulership had, of course, already made themselves felt in the Hellenistic monarchies and in the Roman Empire, but it is Byzantium that exemplifies the theory of absolutism *par excellence*. Although unlike the pagan sovereigns of antiquity the Christian Byzantine emperors could not claim to be worshipped as divinities, they did play to the full their role as God's deputy on earth. Surrounded by all the splendor and luxury of the imperial palaces, decked in silk brocade and bejewelled golden ornaments, the emperors of Byzantium inspired the awe and envy of the world.

Yet any man might become basileus; lowly birth was no bar to the throne, for God's hand could select His chosen one from any walk of life. Dynasties before the seventh century had invariably lasted only two or three generations; then indeed, the old pattern seemed to be changing, for since Heraclius of Carthage seized the throne in 610, his descendants had succeeded in an unbroken, orderly line. Still, what God had given, God might take away. . . .

Practically no Byzantine would have questioned the idea

that the hand of God moved in history, for religion was a very real force in the Byzantine world, an element of vital importance in the daily lives of everyone from the basileus down to his poorest subjects. Icons of Christ and the saints could be found in almost every home, a perennial reminder of the nearness of the unseen world. Miracles, signs and portents, dreams foretelling the future—all were common enough occurences in this environment where the orthodox Christian faith was inextricably interwoven with popular superstition and legend.

Because orthodoxy mattered so much to the Byzantine people, and because the immediate enemies of the early Empire were largely non-Christian (or at least non-orthodox), it comes as no surprise that the emperors capitalized on their role as defenders of Christendom. In the Early Middle Ages, with the great days of the Western monarchies yet to dawn, Byzantium was indisputably the one great Christian power. At a time when much of Western Europe was overrun by Germanic tribesmen and eventually imperial authority disappeared in most of these areas, the Empire in the East with its great capital at Constantinople stood firm. The popes in Old Rome on the far western fringe of the Empire, the kings of the barbarian West, monks in cloisters as far away as Britain—all dated important events by the reigns of the emperors in Constantinople. Diminished though its territorial sway might be, Constantinople was still the center of the world in the mind of the Early Middle Ages.

The imperial city, whose population throughout most of the medieval epoch is estimated at about one million inhabitants, was a bustling metropolis. It was the first Emperor Constantine who had transformed the small seaside town of Byzantium into his capital in A.D. 330 and given it his name. He had chosen an excellent site. Surrounded on three sides by water—the Sea of Marmora to the south, the Bosphoros to the east, and the vast natural harbor of the Golden Horn to the north—Constantinople was on the crossroads of east-west trade, and goods (including many luxury items) from the far corners of the world would be bought and sold in its market places for centuries. The geographic location of the city, more-

over, rendered it easily defensible, and the excellent fortifications built by the early emperors would prove their worth on
innumerable occasions.

It was fortunate indeed that Byzantium possessed such a
strategically located capital, for throughout the Empire's long
history, it was the strength of the capital that time and again
assured the survival of the state. The seventh-century Empire
—into which Justinian II was born and over which he would
eventually rule—was a state beset by frequent crises. More
than by any other single factor, the Mediterranean world of
the seventh century was shaken by the sudden and rapid rise
of Islam. It was in the reign of Justinian II's great-great-grandfather, Heraclius of Carthage, that the followers of the Prophet
Mohammed first rode out of the Arabian desert to launch the
conquests that have affected the course of Near Eastern history
from that day to this. The Byzantine state, exhausted by a
long and devastating war with Persia, the ancient foe of the
Roman Empire, was ill prepared for these incursions of the
Moslems. The Emperor Heraclius had spent much of his reign
in the struggle against Persia, and although ultimately he had
led his troops to complete victory over this ancient enemy, it
was only at the cost of a heavy financial drain and tremendous
losses of men and materials. The invasions of a new foe, the
Moslems, so soon thereafter, were almost too much for the
weakened Byzantine Empire. Heraclius, moreover, who had
been an outstanding military commander in earlier years, was
growing old; burdened down by many ills, physical and men-
tal, he had lost the dynamic leadership ability that had once
made him the hero of his people.

Still the Byzantines under Heraclius and under his descendants would put up a gallant fight against the Arab invaders,
though for a long time it was to be a losing one. In the middle
years of the seventh century several of the finest provinces of
the Empire slipped irrevocably into Moslem hands: the Holy
Land, Syria, Egypt; while Asia Minor, the heartland of the
Byzantine state, became prey to almost annual incursions by
Moslem raiders. Not even Constantinople itself was immune
from danger, and Justinian in his childhood was to witness the

great five-year Arab siege of the imperial capital city. Though his father, Constantine IV, at length succeeded in crushing this attempt to destroy the core of the Empire, the problem of Arab aggression by no means disappeared. Throughout Justinian II's reign and for years thereafter, Byzantium time and again would be placed on the defensive against the followers of the Prophet.

But if the Arabs were a formidable foe, an equally serious threat to the well-being of the Byzantine state was posed by the infiltration of barbarian Slavic tribes into the Balkans. This situation was complicated still further when around the middle of the seventh century, Bulgars, originally from central Asia, began to appear in the lands immediately north of the Danube, then to infiltrate southward across the great river that in theory marked the Empire's boundary. In spite of their completely different ethnic background, Bulgars and Slavs would prove to be natural allies in the struggle to wrest the Balkan territories from Byzantine control. Relatively few details are known of Byzantium's counter-efforts against the "Sklavinians" and the Bulgars during these troubled times, but we do know that when the young emperor Justinian II undertook to restore Byzantine authority in "Sklavinia," he was following a course pursued with varying success by his father and grandfather before him. The very scantiness of the source materials reveals something of the gravity of the situation in the areas of the Empire so affected: although unquestionably there were some records that have subsequently disappeared, it was obviously a time in which relatively little history was being written, for the grim realities of life permitted little leisure for scholarly pursuits.

On other frontiers of the Empire lurked other enemies. Italy, once the heartland of the Roman world, was to the seventh-century Byzantine emperors a remote and restless province, difficult to control, both because of the presence of Germanic Lombard invaders and the growing rift between eastern and western Christianity. An imperial governor, the Exarch of Italy, ruled on the emperor's behalf from headquarters in the north-Italian town of Ravenna on the Adriatic coast, and the popes in Old Rome maintained fairly close connections with the imperial court in Constantinople, but these factors notwithstanding, Byzantium's hold on Italy was weak. Even more tenuous was its hold on North Africa, the very area to which Justinian II's dynasty traced its origin. Continually prey to Moslem raids, the North African coast was gradually slipping from Byzantine control, and even in many areas still officially Byzantine, Berber tribesmen exercised the real authority. In the Asiatic areas of the Empire were yet other barbaric tribes pressing their way toward Byzantine territory, among them, in the lands to the north of the Black Sea, the Khazars, whose fortunes were one day to be strangely linked with those of Justinian II.

Against all such enemies, real and potential, stood the Empire, guardian of the heritage of classical civilization and of the Christian faith, heir and continuator of ancient Rome. From Septum of North Africa opposite the coast of Spain to Cherson of the Crimea on the shores of the Black Sea stretched the far-flung imperial domain. Rocked by crises though she might be, Byzantium was still a formidable power. Her losses, it was believed, were temporary; territories which had fallen into other hands stood in open defiance of their only rightful sovereign, the emperor in Constantinople. Such was the Byzantine viewpoint, and so it was that Justinian II, like many another Byzantine ruler before and after him, could describe himself as basileus of the *oikoumenē*—emperor of the whole inhabited earth.

Represented among the diverse peoples who inhabited the Byzantine state was a vast conglomeration of ethnic backgrounds and languages. As subjects of the emperor, they could all speak of themselves as Romans; for indeed, through the centuries, the official name of the Byzantine state was always Romanía, the Roman Empire. But pride themselves though they might on the name of Roman, knowledge of Latin was rapidly disappearing in the seventh-century Empire, except in its far western reaches. Greek was the official language of the court; it was the language that Justinian II and his family spoke as their native tongue, though their ancestor Heraclius,

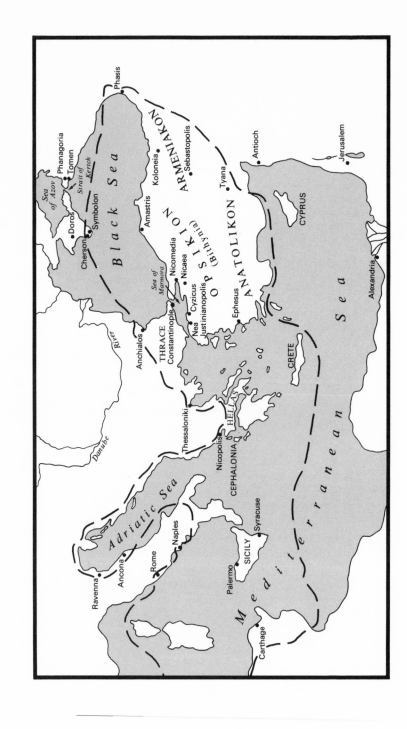

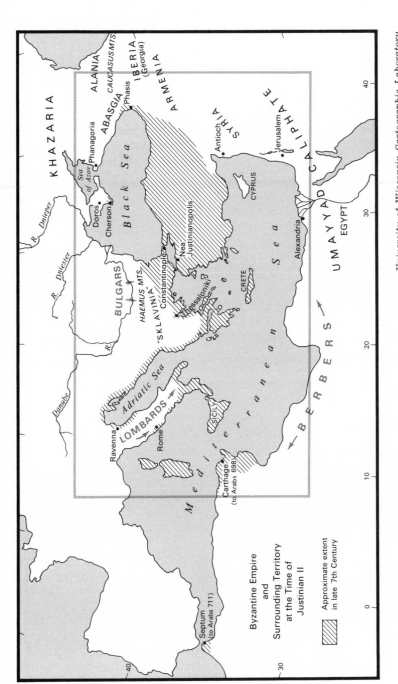

Byzantine Empire
and
Surrounding Territory
at the Time of
Justinian II

Approximate extent
in late 7th Century

the founder of the dynasty (who was himself a man of Carthage in North Africa), was reputedly of Armenian descent.[1]

While most scholars accept the Armenian lineage of the Heraclian dynasty, there must have also existed other roots of the family tree to produce the famous golden hair that was a distinguishing characteristic of Heraclius and most of his descendants. We know little or nothing of the ethnic background of the women who married into the Heraclian family, but in all probability, Justinian II's ancestry was as diverse as that of many of his subjects.

Amidst this great diversity in the background of various subject peoples, the Byzantine Empire found its strongest unifying force in the Christian faith. The importance of religion in the thinking of the Byzantine people has already been pointed out; compounded with this was a passion for theological dispute that mirrors the ancient Greeks' love of philosophical debate, and yet in its very intensity is difficult for most moderns to comprehend. In the seventh-century Christian world, there was as yet only one officially recognized church; the final schism of Roman Catholic and Eastern Orthodox was still several centuries in the future, though the points of dispute leading to that eventual result were already becoming manifest. In a world where precise acceptance of "correct" beliefs and practices was considered a matter of first-rate importance, most Byzantine· emperors devoted considerable attention and study to matters of theology, and Justinian II would be no exception. Some of the most vivid glimpses we have of daily life and customs at this time come from the enactments of Justinian's Quinisext Council in its efforts to improve the moral standards and to regularize the liturgical practices of the Byzantine people.

But if in the area of theology Justinian fulfilled the usual Byzantine expectation of an emperor concerned for the religious well-being of his subjects, in certain other areas he was far from conforming to the prototype of a typical Byzantine sov-

[1] Evidence on Heraclius's ancestry is most fully set out in Henri Grégoire, "An Armenian Dynasty on the Byzantine Throne," *Armenian Quarterly* 1 (1946): 4–21.

ereign. Justinian was an innovator: his ideas were often ahead of his contemporaries; and as an absolute monarch he was prepared to ride roughshod over entrenched traditions that stood in his way. Only through careful historical detective work can the modern scholar begin to evaluate his very real contributions to the development of the Byzantine state, for as will be seen, most of the detailed early sources we possess come from a tradition hostile to his memory. The clues that lead to reconstruction of a record of his constructive statesmanship are in their own way as intriguing as Justinian's own strange adventures, and certainly are as much a part of his story.

2

PROBLEMS OF THE SOURCES

HISTORY has played many strange tricks on the individuals who have helped to make it. The whole matter of what information survives for historians to work with and how they then interpret it is a hazardous proposition at best. When source materials are either scarce or intensely biased or both, the process of historical interpretation becomes the more difficult, as the case of Justinian II plainly shows.

There were unquestionably people writing history in the Byzantine Empire in the days of Justinian II and the emperors immediately after him.[1] The problem is: not any of these works survive. It is not until almost a hundred years later, near the close of the eighth century, that we find extant detailed narratives of the life and reigns of Justinian *Rhinotmetos* ("Justinian with the cut-off nose"), and then, from about the same period, come two chronicles, the works of Nikephoros the Patriarch[2]

[1] At least one of these historians is known by name: Traianos the Patrician, mentioned by the Byzantine lexicographer Suidas as having "flourished under Justinian Rhinotmetos." See Edwin Patzig, "Leo Grammaticus und seine Sippe," *Byzantinische Zeitschrift* 3 (1894): 471; also Karl Krumbacher, *Geschichte der byzantinischen Litteratur von Justinian biz zum Ende des oströmischen Reiches,* 2d ed. (Munich, 1897), p. 104.

[2] Nikephoros of Constantinople, *Opuscula Historica,* ed. Carolus de Boor (Leipzig, 1880). This work is also known as the *Brevarium.* Nikephoros became Patriarch of Constantinople in 806, but probably composed his chronicle some years earlier. For details see Paul J. Alexander, *The Patriarch Nicephorus of Constantinople* (Oxford, 1958), pp. 157–62.

and Theophanes the Confessor.[3] These authors wrote independently of each other, but both utilized earlier material now lost. Consequently, since Nikephoros and Theophanes are the best extant sources we have, subsequent interpretation of Justinian II from Byzantine times to the present has largely depended on them. And since both chroniclers depict Justinian as a ruthless tyrant, so obsessed by the drive for vengeance as to forget the serious responsibilities of emperorship, writers ever since have tended to accept this interpetation without sufficient scrutiny.[4]

Yet there are several reasons why Justinian II deserves a fairer hearing, or to put it another way, why one cannot believe literally every word that Nikephoros and Theophanes wrote. The first of these might be called the Case of Historiographical Hostility. We know that it is not uncommon in history to find that when a monarch has fallen from his throne and a new dynasty is installed, writers of the new regime make a diligent effort to malign the memory of the vanquished foe. King Richard III of England is perhaps the most famous victim of such systematic defamation. Though admittedly the particulars of Richard's case differ considerably from Justinian's, a somewhat comparable bias seems to pervade the writings of Nikephoros and Theopanes in the sections of their chronicles dealing with this emperor, bias which they derived, no doubt, from their "lost sources." And although virtually nothing is known of these lost sources, there are clues which suggest why they should have been concerned to picture Justinian in such unfavorable terms.

First of all, it appears that the Patriarch Nikephoros used only one source for the section of his chronicle which includes Justinian, but that this source was very close to Justinian's own

[3] Theophanes, *Chronographia*, ed. Carolus de Boor, 2 vols. (Leipzig, 1883; reprint ed., Hildesheim, 1963), vol. 1.

[4] There has never been a full-length modern biographical study of Justinian II. The only significant secondary work devoted exclusively to his life and reigns is a lengthy essay by Charles Diehl, "L'Empereur au nez coupé," *Revue de Paris* 30 (1923): 71–94. Diehl's work, while important as a pioneering study of Justinian, largely presents the chroniclers' accounts at their face value and its overall characterization of the emperor is of the most unfavorable sort.

lifetime, and as such, based on living memory of the events it records. An intricate textual study of one of the early surviving manuscripts of the patriarch's work has even revealed that the precise date of Nikephoros's "lost source" was 713, the year in which Justinian's successor, Philippikos Vardan, lost his throne.[5] Although this "713 Chronicle" concluded with a description of Vardan's fall from power, in all likelihood most of it was prepared during Vardan's reign and reflected the "official" view that Justinian had fallen because of his many misdeeds and that Vardan, who played so large a role in the *coup* that dethroned him, was justified in doing so. Nevertheless, because of its proximity to Justinian's lifetime, the narrative which Nikephoros drew from the 713 Chronicle is probably largely accurate, and when due notice is taken of its bias it remains an extremely valuable source of information.

Somewhat longer and more detailed than Nikephoros's work is the *Chronographia* of Theophanes. Now, a careful scrutiny of the two accounts reveals that Theophanes is far more prejudiced against Justinian's memory than is Nikephoros. At almost every turn, he enlarges upon the unfavorable incidents reported by his contemporary; and in some instances adds data, usually of the most adverse sort, which have no parallel at all in Nikephoros's work. Unless we are to assume that Theophanes simply fabricated these details out of his imagination (a most unlikely hypothesis in light of the care with which Byzantine historians generally repeated their source materials), the reason for Theophanes' intensely unfavorable portrait of Justinian must lie in the "lost sources" that were used by him and not by Nikephoros. If only we could know what these lost sources were and when they were written! But unfortunately we do not know with absolute certainty. Nevertheless, there is a surprising amount of evidence for the hypothesis that the growth of a "black legend" of Justinian II belongs to the reign of the Emperor Leo III.

Leo ascended the Byzantine throne in 717, six years after

[5] Louis Orosz, *The London Manuscript of Nikephoros' "Brevarium"* (Budapest, 1948), pp. 3–12.

Justinian's death. These six years had been a period of virtual anarchy for the Empire; the three emperors who reigned between Justinian and Leo had been deposed in rapid succession. Moreover, while the internal administration of the state tottered, the problems of Arab and Slavic invasions were growing ever more serious. It was scarcely a period which would encourage the production of extensive historical writing. Leo III, on the other hand, managed to restore stable government to the Empire, and his great victory over the Arab besiegers of Constantinople at the beginning of his reign effectively eased the pressures of Saracen invaders for years to come.

Granted that this restoration of order provides an atmosphere probably more conducive to such scholarly pursuits as the writing of history, the question next needs to be raised of what can be known of the Emperor Leo's personal opinions concerning his predecessor, Justinian II, since these may well have colored the accounts of him produced during Leo's reign. Several very significant items need to be noticed here. First, as Theophanes relates in a section which will be examined in some detail in a later chapter, Leo had sound reason for hating the memory of Justinian, for rightly or wrongly he was convinced that Justinian had once attempted to have him killed.[6] Nor is Leo's personal ill will the only factor that may have influenced the historical interpretation of Justinian II at this time. Justinian, as will be noted, was a fervent promoter of the veneration of icons. When Leo undertook to enforce the new policy of inconoclasm, it would naturally be a blow to the party that favored the icons if one of their noted adherents were depicted in highly unfavorable terms. Finally, at least once during Leo's reign, a pretender arose who claimed to be Justinian's son, Tiberius.[7] This particular individual, who was "discovered" by a Byzantine but sponsored by the Arabs, never posed a serious threat to Leo's throne. Yet the fact that such

[6] Theophanes, pp. 391–95.

[7] Reported by Gregorius Abû'l Faraj Bar Hebraeus, *Chronography*, trans. from Syriac by Ernest A. Wallis Budge, 2 vols. (Oxford, 1932), 1:110. Bar Hebraeus was a thirteenth-century chronicler whose work undoubtedly was based on earlier sources.

an attempt was made at all indicates that its promoters hoped
they could count on some dynastic loyalty to the House of
Heraclius among the Byzantine people. The Emperor Leo may
well have felt that anti-Justinian propaganda was a helpful
measure in squelching the aspirations of anyone who might
claim the throne as the fallen monarch's heir.

Thus it seems likely that with the passing of years, more
and more tales of misgovernment began to cluster about the
name of Justinian II. These materials, while lacking in Nikephoros's 713 source, were found in other sources used by
Theophanes, and the final result is the portrait of the bloodthirsty and almost mad emperor emerging from the pages of
his *Chronographia*. In attempting to reinterpret Justinian II,
frequent notice will be taken of items traceable only to Theophanes, which seem to reveal plainly the growth of historiographical hostility against the fallen emperor.

Nor is this presumed development of an anti-Justinian
legend the only reason why he is entitled to a fairer hearing.
From a variety of scattered and sometimes seemingly unlikely
sources come clues revealing him in a different light. In subsequent chapters, notice will be taken of a number of incidents
pointing toward his constructive statesmanship and genuine
concern for the empire over which he ruled. In a few instances,
evidence has even come to light proving Theophanes' asser-
tions to be ill-founded. And even in Theophanes' and Nikephoros's own chronicles are suggestions of the more positive
side of Justinian's accomplishments. All this evidence, weighed
together, does a great deal to discredit the image of Justinian
II as a capricious and fiendish tyrant.

Yet the reinterpreter must also beware of the peril of
whitewashing Justinian's mistakes. His very hot temper and
his sometimes unwise decisions and policies are a part of the
historical record, not to be denied. Although he was a ruler
of considerable ability and intelligence, and most richly
endowed with the gift of courageous persistence, he was sorely
lacking in the level-headed patience and forbearance that he
would have had to possess to have earned a place among
Byzantium's truly great and successful emperors.

3

HEIR APPARENT
669–685

THERE is no exact knowledge of either the precise date or the place of Justinian II's birth, so poorly preserved are the records from that time. For some strange reason, the inhabitants of Cyprus in later centuries claimed him as a native of that island,[1] but since Cyprus was apparently in the hands of the Arabs when Justinian was born, the tradition is in all probability groundless. Much more likely, Justinian's birth occurred in Constantinople, in the porphyry-lined chamber where it was generally arranged that imperial children be born, that they might be literally "born-in-the-purple" and bear the title of Porphyrogenitus. Of his mother, the Empress Anastasia, little is known; she was probably very young when Justinian was born, as her husband, Constantine IV, was only seventeen. And if Constantine had followed the usual imperial custom in selecting his bride, Anastasia must have belonged to a high-ranking family of the Byzantine nobility. Byzantine emperors simply did not marry foreigners in those days, and would not until Justinian himself grew up and shattered the tradition.

[1] This tradition is recorded by the scholarly tenth-century emperor Constantine VII Porphyrogenitus, who accepted it as authentic in his book *De Administrando Imperio*, ed. Gy. Moravcsik, trans. R. J. H. Jenkins (Washington, 1967), pp. 224–25. Sir George Hill, *A History of Cyprus*, 3 vols. (Cambridge, 1940), 1:280n5, denounces it as "absurd."

Some time after Justinian's arrival, another child was born to Constantine and Anastasia, and to this second son, the emperor gave the dynastic name of Heraclius. So far as we know, Heraclius was Justinian's only brother, and if there were any girls in the family, no record of their existence has been preserved.

Among the circle who surrounded the young princes, certainly two of their most esteemed comrades must have been their young uncles, Heraclius and Tiberius, only a few years older than themselves. Sons of the late emperor Constantine III ("Constans") and brothers of Constantine IV, Heraclius and Tiberius both held the honorary title of Co-Emperor. Constantine, who was very jealous of his authority, watched his brothers closely as they grew to maturity, lest they display signs of undue ambition.

Although we have no direct knowledge of what education the imperial children received in this era, we can be sure, in view of the high value which the Byzantines traditionally attached to learning, that the emperor's sons were carefully tutored. Young Justinian certainly heard a great deal of the history of his own dynasty: of his great-great-grandfather, Heraclius of Carthage, who had waged successful war against the Persians only to be defeated by the Moslems and to die in utter despair; of Heraclius's frail son, Heraclius-Constantine,[2] who reigned for only a few months but left behind him a strong young son to carry on the dynasty. This son—Justinian's grandfather—was the brilliant, erratic Constantine III (or "Constans," as he was generally called), who for years had carried on the struggle against Islam and then suddenly

[2] Considerable diversity of practice exists among historians in their naming of the two emperors whom I have called respectively Heraclius-Constantine and Constantine III (Constans). In some works, the former is known as Constantine III and the latter as Constans II. Such confusion originated in the extremely limited source material of the time, but numismatic evidence indicates beyond any doubt that Heraclius-Constantine used both names officially and that his son (though apparently he was usually called by the diminutive "Constans") was legally named Constantine and always used that name on his coinage. Thus Constans and not his father is the real Constantine III.

decided to leave Constantinople and relocate the seat of imperial government in Syracuse on the island of Sicily. Justinian must have learned, too, the chilling tale of his grandfather's murder: only about a year before Justinian was born, an attendant of the Emperor Constans attacked him in his bath and struck him a fatal blow on the head with a marble soapdish. This was the turn of events that had brought Justinian's own father, Constantine IV, to the throne at the age of sixteen.

When he received word from Sicily of his father's murder, young Constantine very sensibly had decided to restore Constantinople as the seat of imperial government. The excellent geographic location of the city, surrounded on three sides by water, combined with the towering, heavily fortified walls on the landward side to render it virtually impregnable. Nevertheless the Arabs, whose incursions into the Empire were growing yearly more daring and successful, sooner or later were certain to attempt an attack on the capital. Little Prince Justinian was five years old when it began: the Arab fleet appeared in the waters around Constantinople for the first time in the spring of 674. Through the summer the city remained under siege, though with the coming of cold weather the enemy sailed off to their base at Cyzicus. Nonetheless the Arabs were not easily discouraged, and for four more years the return of spring brought with it the return of the Arab fleet to Constantinople. Various naval encounters took place in the waters near the capital, in which Byzantine ships, armed with their new secret weapon, the mysterious "Greek fire" which burned on water, wrought havoc amongst their Arab foes. It is altogether likely that young Justinian watched some of these battles from the sea walls of the city, and learned from firsthand observation the determined persistence of the enemy.

It was not until after repeated reversals that the Caliph Muawiya finally consented in 678 to a humiliating peace treaty, under the terms of which he agreed to send the emperor three thousand pieces of gold, fifty slaves, and fifty horses, annually for the next thirty years.[3]

[3] F. Dölger, *Regesten der Kaiserurkunden des oströmischen Reiches*, 5 vols. (Munich, 1924), 1:28.

Constantine IV, still in his twenties, had accomplished one of the most crucial victories in Western history; he had saved the strongest Christian city in the world of his day from Moslem conquest, and by so doing, had halted the Moslem advance into southeastern Europe that would have surely taken place had Constantinople fallen. History in the Western tradition has little to say of Constantine IV, yet were it not for him, all Europe might be Moslem today.

But if he had reached the pinnacle of outward success, all was not peaceful within the imperial family. Constantine, eager to secure the undisputed succession for his son Justinian, watched the ambitions of his brothers Heraclius and Tiberius with growing alarm.

There is little hint, however, of the rising tensions in Constantine's household in the family portrait of the emperor, his brothers, and the young prince Justinian preserved on a wall of the Church of Sant'Apollinare-in-Classe in Ravenna (Figure 1). This mosaic, which has undergone considerable restoration, commemorates Constantine's bestowal of certain ecclesiastical privileges on the church of Ravenna and depicts the emperor handing a scroll, marked in large letters PRIVILEGIA, to the dignitaries of the Ravenna church. It is interesting that Constantine is dressed in garb almost exactly like that worn by his hero Justinian I in another, more famous, Ravenna mosaic from the Church of San Vitale. Like Justinian I in the earlier work, Constantine wears a cloak of purple and gold over a plain white tunic, while on his feet are the red shoes that were a distinctive symbol of imperial status. In one respect, however, the later emperor's costume differs considerably from the model of Justinian I, for Constantine wears no crown or other headgear. His longish golden hair is neatly combed in what later ages would call the page-boy style, while his thin face is impassive and calm.

At Constantine's right stand his two brothers, Heraclius and Tiberius, the co-emperors, and although the artists accorded them as well as Constantine the stereotyped haloes that distinguish emperors in Byzantine art, they are clothed not

FIGURE 1

Mosaic in the Church of Sant'Apollinare in Classe, Ravenna, showing, from left to right: Justinian II as a young prince, Co-Emperors Heraclius and Tiberius (brothers of Constantine IV), the Emperor Constantine IV (father of Justinian), the Archbishop of Ravenna, and other dignitaries
Courtesy of the Church of Sant'Apollinare in Classe

anywhere so splendidly as their brother; and their shoes, instead of imperial red, are plain black.

Next to his uncle Heraclius stands the Prince Justinian. Although the artists certainly erred in giving him the height of a full-grown man, his features and clothing clearly indicate that this is the portrait of a young boy. Clad in a short brown tunic with elaborate embroidery on the sleeves and around the skirt, Justinian stands clutching a model church building, symbolizing, no doubt, his father's benefactions to the bishopric of Ravenna. The young prince's legs are encased in white stockings, and on his feet are black shoes with pointed toes exactly like those worn by his uncles. A small circlet indicating his princely rank rests on his light brown hair. He is a handsome boy, in spite of the fact that his youthful gaze stares out at the world with a somewhat furtive expression, almost as if he were aware that beneath the outward facade of imperial harmony, trouble was brewing.

The storm broke suddenly and violently when Justinian was was about twelve. Although the details are vague and confused,[4] it appears that Constantine's first decisive act against his brothers was to deprive them of their imperial titles, though they were still to be known as his "divinely protected brothers." This demotion precipitated a revolt on behalf of Heraclius and Tiberius among the troops stationed in Anatolia. Basing their plea for reinstatement of the imperial brothers on the idea that the heavenly Trinity should be reflected in an earthly trinity of emperors, the leaders of the revolt sought audience with Constantine, who conferred with them, then sentenced them to immediate execution. For Heraclius and Tiberius themselves, Constantine decreed the sentence of *rhinokopia*, the cutting off or mutilation of their noses. This penalty was designed to destroy forever their claims to the throne, for to be emperor, the Byzantines believed, a man must be free of any serious, noticeable physical blemish or imperfection.

[4] The best study of the entire problem is that of E. W. Brooks, "The Brothers of the Emperor Constantine IV," *English Historical Review* 30 (1915): 42–51.

FIGURE 2
Constantine IV; coin of his reign, 668–685
Dumbarton Oaks Collection

We have no knowledge of what Justinian may have
thought of his father's decision to inflict *rhinokopia* upon his
two young uncles. One thing is certain, however: with his
own nose as yet intact, the heir apparent could scarcely have
dreamed that one day he would himself overturn the tradition
barring such "defectives" from the imperial throne.

At this point, perhaps, we need to take a further look at
the practice of judicial mutilation, which is undoubtedly one
of the most repellent features of Byzantine civilization. How
could it be, the modern reader tends to ask (without pausing
to reflect on his own civilization) that refined, civilized, and
professedly Christian people could consent to the deliberate
mutilation of individuals—amputation of noses, ears, or other

parts of human anatomy, or (as also took place on some occasions) the blinding of eyes? Savage as these practices may appear, it is important to remember that the ethical system of the Early Middle Ages deemed judicial mutilation a merciful substitute for the death penalty, and could even quote the scriptural admonition "If thy right hand offend thee, cut it off" as proof text for this point of view. In cases involving unsuccessful contenders for the imperial throne, a sentence of mutilation was considered particularly useful, because of the widespread belief that the emperor must be a perfect physical specimen.

Since one of Constantine IV's major motives in the ouster of his brothers was to secure the undisputed succession for Justinian, many writers from Byzantine times to the present have assumed that he then elevated his young son to the rank of co-emperor.[5] There is, however, no concrete evidence to support such an assertion; there are no coins picturing Constantine and Justinian together, which certainly would have appeared had Justinian actually been crowned in his father's lifetime.[6] Constantine, after all, was still young, and his son but a child; and he probably felt the ceremony would best be postponed a few years. Perhaps he hesitated, too, over what to do about his second son, Heraclius.

From the year 684 comes an incidental glimpse of a lesser imperial ceremony which is an interesting sidelight on one of

[5] This mistaken concept stems from Theophanes, who reports (p. 360) that after the removal of his two brothers, "Constantine reigned alone with Justinian his son." For details see Ernst Kornemann, *Doppelprinzipat und Reichsteilung im Imperium Romanum* (Leipzig, 1930), pp. 164–65, which shows that the claim for Justinian's co-regency is ungrounded.

[6] A further clue that Justinian was never co-emperor with his father comes from a document issued by him on February 17, 687, and dated in the "second year" of his reign. Since emperors included in their regnal years any period of co-emperorship, this document supplies conclusive proof that Justinian could not have been named co-emperor before February, 685. Constantine died in July, 685.

the customs of the time.[7] In that year, Constantine IV, who studiously cultivated the good will of the papacy, sent a valuable package to Pope Benedict II in Rome; and when the imperial gift arrived, the pope, accompanied by "the clergy and army of Rome," marched out to receive it with full ceremony. The contents of the package were two locks of hair, snipped from the heads of the emperor's two sons. These tokens signified that the princes Justinian and Heraclius were to be looked upon as "spiritual sons" of the pope.[8]

This ceremony of spiritual adoption is the last we hear of Justinian's brother Heraclius, and it is altogether possible that he died soon thereafter.

In the following year, 685, death came suddenly and unexpectedly to Constantine IV, the result of an attack of dysentery. He was only thirty-three. Justinian, his undisputed successor, was sixteen—and in Byzantine eyes, a youth of sixteen was a man fully grown. Thus, unready as he may have been for the full responsibilities of sovereignty, the young emperor Justinian II would be determined from the start not only to reign but to rule.

[7] Reported by the anonymous chronicler of the *Liber Pontificalis*, ed. L. Duchesne, 3 vols. (Paris, 1955), 1:363. The sections of the *Liber Pontificalis* dealing with the reigns of Constantine IV and Justinian II are contemporaneous with the events they describe.

[8] From Western Europe at approximately this same period comes an interesting example of this same practice: Charles Martel sent a lock of his son Pepin's hair to Liutprand, King of the Lombards, as a token of spiritual adoption. Duchesne, *Liber Pontificalis*, 1:364n.

4

JUSTINIAN, THE ARABS, AND
THE SLAVS

WHAT was he like—this teen-
aged boy so suddenly exalted to the highest position in the
world of his era? The coins of the first year of his reign give
us a good indication of his physical appearance (Figure 3):
the beardless face beneath the imperial diadem is almost child-
like in its youthfulness, yet his hollow cheeks and very pointed
chin lend a certain air of distinction to his features. According
to the fashion of the times, his hair, carefully curled, hangs
long around his ears and is clipped in short bangs across his
forehead. Within a year after his accession, he would grow a
small, neat beard, and the dies of his coinage would be altered
accordingly (Figure 4).

As far as his personality is concerned, all evidence indicates that he was a young man of considerable self-assurance.
Undeniably intelligent and possessed of a genuine interest in
affairs of state, young Justinian gave promise of being a
dynamic sovereign, and if his youth was against him, it was
to be remembered that his father Constantine had also been
very young when he succeeded to the throne. Like the great
emperor whose name he bore, Justinian II had a passion for
building and a deep interest in theology, but quite contrary
to his namesake (who avoided personal participation in military exploits), he was eager to win glory for himself on the

battlefield. In this respect he was a true son of the Heraclian House: it was the dynasty's founder, Heraclius of Carthage, who had revived the old Roman tradition of the emperor as personal commander of his forces in the field, a practice that Justinian's more immediate predecessors had continued.

Almost certainly someone pointed out to the new emperor at his accession that never before in the long history of the Roman Empire had one family retained possession of the throne unto the fifth generation, and now the house of Heraclius, in the person of Justinian II, had accomplished this feat. It was a pleasant realization, this awareness that the Heraclians seemed destined to reign forever, and certainly the thought of it contributed to Justinian's already abundant self-confidence.

There is no record of Justinian's coronation, but following the long-accepted custom, it must have been performed by the Patriarch of Constantinople in the beautiful church of Hagia Sophia.

Since Byzantine ceremonial practically demanded the presence of an empress as well as an emperor, it was probably early in his reign that Justinian took his first bride. Her name was Eudokia; that is all that is known of her, save for the fact that she bore her husband a little daughter and that she died, still quite young, and was buried in a tomb of rose-colored marble in the Church of the Holy Apostles.[1] The exact year of her death is not recorded, but probably she was alive through most of Justinian's first reign. Even less is known of Eudokia and Justinian's daughter. Not even her name is preserved; and though, as will be seen, years later her father schemed to marry her off to the Khan of the Bulgars, there is no record that this marriage ever took place.

When we turn from Justinian's private life to his public

---

[1] Eudokia's existence is known from none of the literary sources, only from a record of the inscription on her tomb. Philip Grierson, "The Tombs and Obits of the Byzantine Emperors (337–1042)," *Dumbarton Oaks Papers* 16 (1962): 30–32. See also Glanville Downey, "The Tombs of the Byzantine Emperors at the Church of the Holy Apostles in Constantinople," *Journal of Hellenic Studies* 79 (1959): 35.

FIGURE 3
Justinian II at 16; coin of his first reign
Dumbarton Oaks Collection

activities, we find that the sources fortunately become much more informative. His military undertakings in particular receive a great deal of attention from the chroniclers Nikephoros and Theophanes, who in spite of the fact that they scarcely have a good word to say for Justinian in this respect reveal, nonetheless, something of the extent of his ambitions. Other sources help to place Justinian's military policy in clearer perspective and show that his accomplishments were by no means as disastrous as the hostile chroniclers would have us believe.

When the young emperor received a briefing on foreign policy at the time of his accession, his advisors no doubt in-

FIGURE 4
Justinian II at about 19; coin of his first reign
Dumbarton Oaks Collection

cluded among the major areas of concern the Arabs of the Caliphate and the "Sklavinians" in the Balkans. In 685, the Byzantine position vis à vis the Umayyad Caliphate appeared relatively secure; the treaty of 678 still held, and, provided that both sides kept their pledged word, they could look forward to twenty-three more years of peaceful relations before it expired. Conditions in the Arab world, however, had altered considerably since the Caliph Muawiya and Constantine IV had drawn up this arrangement. Old Muawiya was dead now, and the succession to the caliph's throne had fallen into dispute. Abd-al-Malik, who assumed the title of Caliph in the same year that Justinian II became emperor, faced much opposition among his own subjects.[2] As Justinian's advisors must have pointed out, it was an ideal time to expand the Byzantine sphere of influence at Arab expense, and this prospect won the enthusiastic support of the young sovereign.

On the other hand, the Sklavinian situation presented a far more dismal picture. Justinian certainly knew of the unhappy incident in which his father had been involved in 680. Because of increased interference in Balkan affairs by the Bulgar tribesmen from across the Danube, Constantine at that time had prepared a large-scale invasion of the Bulgar homeland, hoping to crush these warlike allies of the Sklavinians and thus, perhaps, to bring the Balkan territories more firmly under imperial control.

As it turned out, however, when the imperial troops debarked in the area north of the Danube, the Bulgar foe refused to appear, much less to give battle. After four days of inactivity, Constantine (who was suffering from gout) departed for home with the announced intention of taking the waters at a health resort. Subordinates were left in command to carry on hostilities against the Bulgar forces when and if they should appear. By the rank and file of the army, however, the Emperor's departure was misconstrued. His "flight" produced a widespread panic, discipline vanished, and then as the confused Byzantines hastened to prepare for their own escape, the Bulgars fell upon them. In the rout that followed, the Bulgars pursued the fleeing Byzantines southward across the Danube into the heartland of Sklavinia, and once there, they refused to leave. Constantine had little choice but to conclude hostilities by granting these newcomers a subsidy; and thus, ironically, much of the annual income from the caliph's tribute was in turn handed over, year by year, to the Khan of the Bulgars. From the Byzantine point of view, it was most humiliating, and it is little wonder that Justinian II hoped to alter the situation.

But first to deal with the Arabs. . . .

    [2] For details see Julius Wellhausen, *The Arab Kingdom and Its Fall*, trans. Margaret Graham Weir (1927; reprint ed., Beirut, 1963), pp. 184–200; Philip K. Hitti, *History of the Arabs*, 3d ed. (New York, 1951), p. 212; *Encyclopedia of Islam*, new ed., s.v. "'Abd al-Malik b. Marwān."

At the far eastern borders of the Empire lay the lands of Armenia and Georgia (or Iberia, as it was then called). Largely independent either of Byzantium or the Caliphate, these territories nonetheless possessed historic ties with the Byzantine domain and yet in recent times had tended toward closer alignment with the Arabs. Now, while the Caliph Abd-al-Malik was beset by rivals for his throne and too busy to intervene effectively, would be the ideal time to restore Byzantine authority in these areas. With this objective in mind, Justinian ordered Leontios, *strategos* (governor and commanding general) of the Anatolikon theme, or military province, to prepare for invasion.[3]

Leontios, an old friend and comrade-in-arms of the late Emperor Constantine, was a skilled militarist, and his Armenian campaign netted considerable plunder for the imperial treasury. The Byzantine advance into Armenia and the surrounding territory, however, did not go unopposed by the Caliphate, and the Arabs seized two Byzantine strongholds in retaliation.[4]

In the meantime, the Byzantines opened offensives against the Caliphate in other areas.[5] Both in North Africa and in Syria, forces of the emperor pushed back the Arab foe with considerable success. At length, in 688/89, the Caliph Abd-al-Malik sued for peace.[6]

The terms of the new treaty are reported in both Arab and

[3] The combination of military and civil authority under *strategoi* in the provinces designated as *themes* is discussed in chapter 11.

[4] Theophanes, p. 363. There is also a report of this campaign, generally in agreement with that of Theophanes, by the eighth-century Armenian chronicler Ghévond, *Histoire des guerres et des conquêtes des Arabes en Arménie*, ed. and trans. Garabed V. Chahnazarian (Paris, 1856), p. 16.

[5] *E. I.*, s.v. "ʿAbd al-Malik"; on North Africa see also *Liber Pontificalis*, 1:366–67; Charles Diehl, *L'Afrique byzantine*, 2 vols. (Paris, 1896; reprint ed. in 1 vol., New York, n.d.), pp. 581–82.

[6] Theophanes, p. 363, causes considerable confusion in placing Justinian's treaty with Abd al-Malik in 685/86, the first year of Justinian's reign; in fact, he reports the treaty before he tells of Leontios's Armenian campaign. Arab sources show clearly that Theophanes' chronology cannot be accepted. See E. W. Brooks, "The Arabs in Asia Minor (641–750) from Arabic Sources," *Journal of Hellenic Studies* 18 (1898): 189.

Byzantine sources, and it is clear that practically every clause represented a gain for Justinian II. The caliph's tribute was increased to one thousand gold pieces, one horse, and one slave payable every Friday.[7] In regard to the disputed territories of Armenia and Iberia, and also the island of Cyprus, a remarkable agreement was worked out, revealing considerable common sense on the part of both the emperor and the caliph. These territories, it was decided, would not be under the direct sovereignty of either power, but would be placed under a condominium arrangement whereby emperor and caliph would share equally their tax revenue. There does not seem to be any clear indication of how long this arrangement remained in force in Armenia and Iberia,[8] but in Cyprus the condominium provision remained in effect for some two hundred and sixty years, providing the island with both local autonomy and unusually stable government. Perhaps it was out of gratitude to the emperor who was to thank for this arrangement that the Cypriots originated the legend that Justinian was himself a native of their island.

It was left to modern scholarship to evaluate the worth of the Cyprus condominium,[9] for the Byzantine chroniclers who report the arrangement do so without a word of praise for Justinian. Another feature of the treaty of 688/89, however, provokes the chroniclers, particularly Theophanes, to say a great deal against Justinian: this is the matter of the Mardaïtes.

The Mardaïtes were a tribe of rugged mountaineers settled along the Arab-Byzantine frontier in the area around and to

[7] Theophanes, p. 363, says the payment was to be made "every day," but compare the Arab chronicler al-Ṭabarî, quoted in Brooks, "The Arabs in Asia Minor," p. 189, who reports much more credibly that a payment was to be made "every assembly day," i.e., Friday. See also Hill, *History of Cyprus,* 1:286n6.

[8] Probably not long, since the Battle of Sebastopolis (692) apparently ended Byzantine authority in these areas. See below, chapter 6.

[9] Particularly R. J. H. Jenkins, "Cyprus between Byzantium and Islam, A.D. 688–965," George E. Mylonas and Doris Raymond, eds., *Studies Presented to David Moore Robinson,* 2 vols. (St. Louis, 1953), 2:1006–14.

the north of Lebanon.[10] Intrepid guerilla fighters, they had sold their services to both caliph and emperor on various occasions. Since his accession to the throne, Justinian II had found them very useful in harassing the Arabs, while Abd-al-Malik had come to consider them highly undesirable neighbors. Consequently, the two sovereigns agreed that Justinian should undertake to transplant twelve thousand of these tribesmen to other locations well inside the Byzantine domain, and not long thereafter, the young emperor is found personally supervising the project of their relocation.[11]

By consenting to transfer the Mardaïtes from their homeland, Theophanes complains, Justinian foolishly destroyed "the brass wall," the buffer zone that had protected the Empire from Arab raids heretofore. "Romanía has suffered dreadful evils from the Arabs even until now," Theophanes laments, all because Justinian moved the Mardaïtes![12]

Yet in reality, the picture is scarcely so bleak as Theophanes paints it. From the historian-emperor Constantine VII (who reigned in the tenth century) comes testimony that the Mardaïte colonies founded by Justinian II were still important bases in the imperial defense structure almost three hundred years later.[13] If he had lost a brass wall in one area, Justinian had gained recruits who would serve the Empire well at other

[10] For data on the Mardaïtes see *Encyclopedia of Islam*, s.v. "Mardaites"; Philip K. Hitti, *History of Syria*, 2d ed. (London, 1957), p. 448; and the important recent article by Matti Moosa, "The Relation of the Maronites of Lebanon to the Mardaites and al-Jarājima," *Speculum* 44 (1969): 597–608.

[11] Theophanes, p. 364. From the Arab chronicler, al-Balâdhuri, it appears, too, that the caliph awarded the Mardaïtes a subsidy to assure their good behavior at this point. For details, see al-Balâdhuri, *The Origins of the Islamic State* (*Kitâb Futûḥ al-Buldân*), trans. Philip K. Hitti (New York, 1916), p. 247. See also Hitti, *Syria*, p. 448.

[12] Theophanes, p. 363.

[13] Constantine VII Porphyrogenitus, *De Cerimoniis Aulae Byzantinae*, ed. J. J. Reiskius, 2 vols. (Bonn, 1829), 1:654. It is also from Constantine VII that we learn where the Mardaïtes were re-established. Apparently Justinian divided them into several groups, retrained them as seamen, and settled some in Nicopolis of Epirus and in the Peloponnesus, others on the island of Cephalonia, and still others in Pamphylia in southern Asia Minor.

points. Moreover, Arab sources make it clear that the entire tribe was not transplanted.[14] There were still numerous Mardaïtes left in their old mountain strongholds after the emperor had removed his twelve thousand; and they would continue to harass the Caliphate for years to come.

Justinian and his contemporaries thus had every reason to consider the treaty of 688/89 an unqualified success for Byzantium. At this period, too, optimism must have been running high with regard to the Balkan situation, for shortly before negotiation of his agreement with the caliph, Justinian had staunchly refused the Bulgars their annual subsidy. Then, assuming personal command of the imperial cavalry, the nineteen-year-old emperor departed for Sklavinia with the objective of reestablishing Byzantine authority particularly in the area around Thessaloniki.

One might expect that so patriotic a move as the refusal of tribute to the barbarian Bulgars would win Justinian commendation from the chroniclers, particularly since his Sklavinian campaign was to turn out very successfully. But no. Nikephoros and Theophanes both take the stand that his breaking of the peace established by Constantine IV was but another indication of his folly and overbearing pride.[15]

Be that as it may, the invasion of Sklavinia, which was apparently launched in the spring or summer of 688, proceeded smoothly for the imperial forces. While no detailed accounts of specific battles have been preserved, the reports of large numbers of Sklavinian prisoners of war are confirmation of imperial success. At the climax of his victorious campaign, Justinian II entered in triumph into the fortified city of Thessaloniki, which had long been a Byzantine enclave, surrounded by Sklavinian-held territory. Several interesting bits of archaeological and artistic data survive connected with the emperor's visit to Thessaloniki, and since we are dealing with a period in which every shred of evidence is of potential value, it is to these matters that we now turn.

[14] Al-Balâdhuri, p. 248; see also Hitti, *History of the Arabs*, p. 205.
[15] Nikephoros, p. 36; Theophanes, p. 364.

5

JUSTINIAN IN THESSALONIKI

T HE seventh century had been hard on Thessaloniki. The heavily fortified outpost some three hundred miles west of Constantinople had once been one of the greatest cities of the Empire, and, in time, would be again; but in the age of the Sklavinian invasions, Thessaloniki had become an isolated Byzantine stronghold in the midst of the barbarian peoples who had swallowed up the surrounding area of Thrace. True, in theory, this area still belonged to the Empire, for the invaders set up no rival administrative machinery, but imperial authority varied from weak to nonexistent in the areas where the barbarians predominated.[1] To the citizens of Thessaloniki, the Sklavinians were in a very real sense the enemy. On several occasions in the seventh century, the city felt the pressures of Sklavinian siege, and according to the anonymous writers who chronicled these events, it was only thanks to repeated miracles by the city's heavenly patron, the warrior St. Demetrius, that Thessaloniki was not completely crushed.

Against this background, it is not difficult to imagine the enthusiasm when news reached the city of Justinian's resounding victories and of his impending visit. In all likelihood, the young emperor entered Thessaloniki amid the joyful adulation

[1] George Ostrogorsky, "Byzantium and the South Slavs," *The Slavonic and East European Review* 42 (1963–64): 3–4.

of his subjects; and, if the theory of a number of art historians
is accepted, memory of the happy occasion was preserved for
many years thereafter in a fresco painted on a wall of the
Church of St. Demetrius. This fresco, eventually covered over
with the decorations of later centuries, was brought to light
again in modern times. Although badly damaged, the picture
has proved of great interest to scholars of Byzantine art, and
has occasioned considerable comment. There is no identifying
inscription to reveal the name of the bearded emperor riding
into the city astride a white horse and accompanied by a group
of attendants, but the fresco indisputably belongs to the pre-
iconoclastic age and to the approximate era when Justinian II
was alive. Since Justinian is known to have visited Thessaloniki personally, he of all the emperors of this period seems
most likely to be the one whom the city would have had occasion to memorialize in this way.[2] Moreover, there is a marked
resemblance between the features of the emperor in the fresco
and the portraits of Justinian on his coinage. To the objection
that the man in the fresco appears considerably older than
Justinian's nineteen years, one scholar has ventured the
intriguing suggestion that the painting was actually done in
his second reign and depicts him more as he looked in later
life.[3] In any event, if the fresco is a portrait of Justinian, it
could help to explain why apparently some memory of him
lived on in the city of St. Demetrius, long after most of the
Empire had forgotten he ever existed, or knew him only as
the villain of Theophanes' *Chronographia*.

That such memory did survive down through the ages

[2] This opinion is championed by Ernst H. Kantorowicz, "The 'King's
Advent' and the Enigmatic Panels in the Doors of Santa Sabina," *The
Art Bulletin* 26 (1944): 216, and has been accepted by many subsequent
scholars. See for example Apostolos P. Vacalopoulis, *A History of Thessaloniki*, trans. T. F. Carney (Thessaloniki, 1963), p. 29. For a completely
different interpretation, however, see James D. Breckenridge, "The 'Long
Siege' of Thessalonika: Its Date and Iconography," *Byzantinische Zeitschrift* 48 (1955): 116–22, which suggests that the figure in question
represents an unidentified saint.

[3] A. A. Vasiliev, "L'Entrée triomphale de l'empereur Justinien II à
Thessalonique en 688," *Orientalia Christiana Periodica* 13 (1947): 364.

in Thessaloniki is witnessed by an inscription dating from
the Palaeologan era, the fourteenth or the fifteenth century,
toward the very end of Byzantium's long history.[4] The inscription, on the silver frame of a mosaic once part of a reliquary
designed to hold "holy oil of St. Demetrius," reads simply thus:

> O great martyr Demetrius! Intercede with God that he
> may help me, thy faithful servant, the earthly Emperor of
> the Romans, Justinian, to vanquish my enemies and sub-
> jugate them beneath my feet.[5]

This is clearly a reference to Justinian II, for there never
was another Emperor Justinian after his time; and the possibility that it refers to Justinian I is negated by the fact that so
far as is known, he was never personally involved in warfare
around Thessaloniki. But what is the point, the reader may
well ask, of a prayer in which a man long dead is made to call
upon Thessaloniki's patron saint? The only logical answer is
to see the piece as a deliberate anachronism, contrived in
memory of the dynamic young emperor who had won such
notable victories for Thessaloniki that his fame still endured
there centuries later. The fact that Justinian's name is associated with that of Thessaloniki's beloved St. Demetrius in this
context is indeed an intriguing hint of the survival of historical
traditions about him differing sharply from those preserved by
Nikephoros and Theophanes.

From the time of Justinian's own visit to Thessaloniki
comes another interesting bit of archaeological evidence: the
text of an edict in which the emperor renders thanks to St.
Demetrius for his recent victories and confers upon the saint's
church the privilege of a *halikē*. This inscription, carved on a
marble tablet, was rediscovered in the late nineteenth century
but was carelessly broken into more than seventy pieces by
the workmen who unearthed it. Subsequently, several scholars

---

[4] This inscription is published, translated, and discussed in A. A.
Vasiliev, "The Historical Significance of the Mosaic of Saint Demetrius at
Sassoferrato," *Dumbarton Oaks Papers* 5 (1950): 31–39.

[5] Ibid., p. 32.

have published their renderings of the reconstructed text,[6] and there has been considerable scholarly disagreement as to what precisely is meant by *halikē* in this instance. It may have been one of the state-operated salt shops whose revenues were now being turned over to the Church of St. Demetrius.[7] On the other hand, *halikē* could designate a true salina or saltpan, somewhere outside of Thessaloniki, which was to be held by the clergy of the church tax free.[8]

In either event, the conferral of the benefit led the writer of the edict to some interesting pronouncements of imperial ideology. While the actual text is no doubt the work of some official, the ideas contained in it must have met with the emperor's approval. There is a strong tone of self-assurance along with the gratitude expressed in the emperor's rendering of thanks to God and St. Demetrius:

> . . . We are convinced that God who has crowned us is always the benevolent champion of our piety and most abundantly grants victories to us. . . . We have come to this city of Thessalonica according to the aid of God who has crowned us. . . . We have obtained the helpful support of the holy great martyr Demetrius in various wars which we had made against his and our own enemies. . . .[9]

Revealing, too, are the epithets attached to the emperor's name. He is "the lord of the whole universe, Flavius Justinianus, the God-crowned and peace-maker Emperor . . . the autocrat peaceable benefactor . . . the faithful Emperor in

[6] The Greek text was published by P. N. Papageorgiou in *Byzantinische Zeitschrift* 17 (1908): 354–60. A. A. Vasiliev, "An Edict of the Emperor Justinian II," *Speculum* 18 (1943): 1–13, made certain textual emendations and included an English translation and commentary. Most recent is Charles Edson's improved text in *Inscriptiones Graecae X*, I, Fasc. 1, 24.

[7] Vasiliev, "Edict of Justinian II," p. 10.

[8] So Henri Grégoire, "Un édit de l'empereur Justinien II," *Byzantion* 17 (1944–45): 120–21.

[9] Vasiliev, "Edict of Justinian II," p. 6; cf. Edson, *I.G. X*, I, Fasc. 1, 24.

Jesus Christ the Lord."[10] The emphasis on peace displayed in these titles is interesting, for if nothing else, it is an indication that Justinian believed at this time that his recently completed campaign would put an effective end to the Sklavinian problem around Thessaloniki.

How justified was the emperor's hope in this regard remains a matter of some dispute. Theophanes reports that on their way back to Constantinople the imperial forces were ambushed by the Bulgars and suffered considerable losses, Justinian himself barely escaping with his life.[11] Since this information is found only in Theophanes and not in the generally more reliable work of Nikephoros, it is open to some doubt, particularly since Justinian *was* ambushed by Bulgar enemies on one occasion in his second reign, and Theophanes may simply have been confused as to when this disaster occurred.

Nevertheless, even if the report is reliable, Justinian still had sound reason to feel that the campaign of 688 held promise for a more stable situation in Thrace, for once hostilities were halted, he undertook the next step in his solution of the Sklavinian question: the relocation of thousands of Sklavinians in Asia Minor. The individuals who were to be transported in this way were mainly prisoners of war and their families, but, interestingly, as word spread of how the emperor planned the foundation of a Sklavinian military colony in Bithynia, many volunteers joined the enterprise,[12] attracted by the prospects of regular service in the imperial army and, perhaps, of land grants in their new location.

As we have seen in the moving of the Mardaïtes and now in the even larger undertaking of moving Sklavinians,

---

[10] Vasiliev, p. 6; Edson, p. 24. The epithet *Flavius*, incidentally, is not actually a proper name but an honorific title adopted by many of the early Byzantine emperors in imitation of Constantine I, whose full name was really Flavius Valerius Constantinus. Justinian II's use of it is probably more immediately attributable to the fact that Justinian I frequently used it.

[11] Theophanes, p. 364.

[12] Nikephoros, p. 36; Theophanes, p. 364.

Justinian was a firm believer in wholesale relocation as a cure for many of the Empire's ills. The Sklavinians he transported may have numbered as many as a hundred thousand.[13] Their removal from Thrace certainly eased the pressures on the native inhabitants of that land, while transplanted in areas of Asia Minor where manpower was desperately needed, their warlike energies could be channeled into the service of the Empire in building defenses against the Arabs.

It is true, of course, that such arbitrary moves no doubt rendered the emperor unpopular with many of the individuals concerned, who had no desire to leave their old homes. Another group who may have also looked with disfavor on Justinian's colonization program was that of the great magnates of Asia Minor. The young emperor was no friend of the traditional aristocracy. It could be that an additional motive for his introducing many thousands of Slavs into Asia Minor was to counter the strength of the land-owning aristocrats and their dependents in this area.[14]

In any event, the colony was founded in Bithynia (or, to give the territory its official name at that time, the Opsikion theme). There a certain patrician Neboulos was commissioned to organize a special corps of Sklavinian mercenaries.

It is in connection with the future of this Sklavinian corps that Theophanes launches one of his gravest charges against Justinian II. When the Arab-Byzantine war of 692 broke out, Theophanes reports, thirty thousand of the Sklavinian special corpsmen were present on the battlefield at Sebastopolis; twenty thousand of them defected to the Arab side, and the Byzantines consequently suffered a grave defeat. The emperor, enraged over this betrayal, Theophanes continues, ordered the execution of the remaining ten thousand Slavs and their families.[15]

A very grave accusation, this; even granted a milieu where no one disputed the sovereign's right to life-and-death

[13] Romilly Jenkins, *Byzantium: The Imperial Centuries* (New York, 1966), p. 52.

[14] Ibid., p. 56.

[15] Theophanes, p. 366.

power over his subjects. Fortunately, however, for Justinian's reputation in this case, there is a whole mass of evidence to counter Theophanes' assertion and to relegate it, almost beyond a doubt, to the realm of the black legend that grew up after the emperor's fall.

First of all, the Patriarch Nikephoros, who possessed, let us recall, the "713 source" from a point close to Justinian's lifetime, has a very different account of the battle of Sebastopolis. According to him, the entire Slavic corps, all thirty thousand of them, deserted to the Arabs, and there is no word of Justinian's reputed revenge.[16] There also exists an eleventh-century Syrian chronicle, written by an individual known as Michael the Syrian who probably had access to sources unavailable to the Byzantine chroniclers. In his report of the battle of Sebastopolis, Michael, like Nikephoros, relates that the entire Slavic corps deserted to the Arab side, and knows nothing of any subsequent massacre by the emperor. Interestingly, Michael also has a much smaller estimate of the size of the corps; according to him there were only about seven thousand of them.[17]

Thus challenged by two independent testimonies, Theophanes' charge may well be called into question. But still further indication of its unreliability arises out of a piece of archaeological evidence. In the late nineteenth century a lead seal was found bearing Justinian's portrait, the date "eighth indiction," and an inscription identifying its possessor as an official of the colony of Slavic mercenaries in Bithynia.[18] The Byzantines frequently employed the practice of dating on the fifteen-year indiction cycle, and if one knows the approximate period in question, such dates can readily be translated into

[16] Nikephoros, p. 37.

[17] *Chronique de Michel le Syrien*, trans. J.-B. Chabot, 3 vols. (Paris, 1899; reprint ed., Brussels, 1963), 2:470.

[18] Gustave Schlumberger, in "Sceau des esclaves [mercenaries] slaves de l'éparchie de Bithynie," *Byzantinische Zeitschrift* 12 (1903): 277, deciphered the inscription on the seal. For further detail see George Ostrogorsky, *History of the Byzantine State*, 2d Engl. ed., trans. Joan Hussey (Oxford, 1968), p. 130n4.

the numbering of the more familiar Christian calendar. Now, the only time the eighth indication occurred in Justinian's first reign was the year 694/95. The seal thus comes from a time two or three years after the battle of Sebastopolis and the emperor's alleged massacre of his Sklavinian colonists. This indisputable evidence of a flourishing Sklavinian corps in Bithynia at a time *after* Theophanes' report would lead us to think they were wiped out assures us almost beyond a doubt that the tale of the emperor's terrible vengeance is without foundation in fact.[19] Though Justinian probably did lose many of his Sklavinians through defection to the Arabs at Sebastopolis, the colonization program in Bithynia survived this blow and continued to play a role in the Empire's defense.

[19] Not all scholars, it must be added, arrive at this conclusion. André Maricq, in "Notes sur les Slaves dans le Péloponnèse et en Bithynie et sur l'emploi de 'Slave' comme apellatif," *Byzantion* 22 (1952): 348–49, believes that Justinian massacred the 10,000 as reported by Theophanes but that this number did not comprise the entire Sklavinian colony and that the seal belonged to an official of those who survived. See also Peter Charanis, "The Transfer of Population as a Policy in the Byzantine Empire," *Comparative Studies in Society and History* 3 (1960–61): 143.

6

THE ARAB-BYZANTINE WAR
OF 692

WHAT caused the Arab-Byzantine war of 692? A few years earlier, as we have seen, Justinian and Abd-al-Malik had agreed to the treaty that included the noteworthy condominium clauses and that seemed to provide a basis for peaceable relations between the Empire and the Caliphate in the future. Yet by 692, the Arabs were loudly asserting that Justinian had broken the treaty, and open warfare between the two powers ensued, culminating in the disastrous battle of Sebastopolis.

As with most wars, there were undoubtedly provocations on the part of both antagonists which led to the outbreak of hostilities: provocations built up from the confidence of both sides in their growing power and recent successes. Unfortunately, the chroniclers Nikephoros and Theophanes had such biased material to work with that they made no real effort to get to the roots of the conflict, and the disarmingly uncomplicated data they present as causes leave many questions unanswered. Justinian broke the treaty, says Nikephoros, because of his hybris, his presumptious pride, that caused him to be overconfident in his Sklavinian mercenaries.[1] Theophanes has more detail: the young emperor, acting with "irrational folly,"

[1] Nikephoros, p. 36.

was motivated to remove a number of Cypriots from their
island homeland to a new colony in Asia Minor. Moreover, the
chronicler continues, there was another provocation, a very
silly one indeed, the matter of how Justinian was offended by
Abd-al-Malik's coinage reform.[2] Both of these reputed causes
deserve detailed consideration.

Justinian's moving of the Cypriots is an established fact,
attested and described in a source contemporary with the
event itself: canon 39 of Justinian's Quinisext Council. This
valuable document presents the emperor's own justification for
relocation of the Cypriots; the Christian inhabitants of the
land, it is stated, continued to suffer indignities from their
Moslem neighbors. They were being moved "because of barbarian attacks" and that they might be freed "from servitude
to the Gentiles."[3]

Although no mention is made of the condominium as
such, it is clear that Justinian felt that this Moslem harass-
ment of Christian Cypriots was sufficient reason for retaliation. There is also a suggestion that agitation for permission to
move came from the Christian Cypriot leaders themselves, for
one source reports that John, the Metropolitan Archbishop of
Cyprus, visited Constantinople, apparently to confer with the
emperor on the matter.[4] The area around Cyzicus in the dis-
trict of the Hellespont, which had been severely underpopu-
lated because of Arab raids in Constantine IV's reign, was
chosen as location for the transplanted colony;[5] there, it was

---

[2] Theophanes, p. 365.

[3] The Greek text of the entire Quinisext proceedings is printed in
Sacrorum Conciliorum Nova et Amplissima Collectio, ed. Johannes Dominicus Mansi (Florence, 1755), vol. 11. Canon 39 is found at col. 961.
Constantine VII quoted this material in his book *De Administrando Imperio*, pp. 224–27.

[4] Constantine VII Porphyrogenitus, *De Administrando Imperio*, pp.
224–25.

[5] Ibid.; see also Hill, *History of Cyprus*, 1:288. Incidentally, Theophanes' assertion, p. 365, that all these Cypriots perished in a storm at sea
and never reached their destination is clearly mistaken, as proven by the
evidence of canon 39 and Constantine VII. This appears to be another
instance of the unreliability of Theophanes' "lost sources."

hoped, the experienced Cypriot seamen would provide valuable additional strength for Byzantine defenses.

Justinian seems to have been particularly interested in the future of this settlement. He proudly bestowed upon it the name of Nea Justinianopolis—the New City of Justinian—and at his Quinisext Council he would take particular care to secure for it special ecclesiastical privileges.[6] Nevertheless, however justified the establishment of Nea Justinianopolis seemed in the emperor's eyes, from the Arab point of view it was a flagrant violation of the condominium, for the removal of tax-paying Cypriots from their homeland naturally would diminish the revenues the Arabs could hope to collect there.

Abd-al-Malik's indignation at Justinian's Cypriot policy thus appears sufficient reason for the outbreak of hostilities between the two sovereigns. Moreover, from Arab sources we learn that by 692, the caliph had triumphed over earlier internal opposition to his rule; secure in his own domain, he no longer felt obliged to stay on the good side of Byzantium as he had when he first came to the throne.[7] The Byzantine historians who place the entire blame for the Arab-Byzantine war of 692 on Justinian tend to overlook the fact that it was the caliph's forces who launched the offensive, crossing the border into Byzantine territory.

But besides Justinian's violation of the condominium and Abd-al-Malik's realization that it was a propitious time to attack his Christian foe, were there other points of difference between the Empire and the Caliphate that played a role in

[6] There is much scholarly dispute over what is meant by the ambiguous statement in canon 39 that the Archbishop of Nea Justinianopolis was to have "the right of Constantinople." It is likely that this phrase contains a textual error and should read "the right of Constantia," i.e., the metropolis of Cyprus. If so, this is merely a further statement of the transfer of the archbishopric from the island to Nea Justinianopolis. For details see Charles Joseph Hefele, *A History of the Councils of the Church from the Original Documents*, trans. William R. Clark, 5 vols. (Edinburgh, 1896), 5:229; John Hackett, *A History of the Orthodox Church of Cyprus* (London, 1901), pp. 41–42.

[7] *Encyclopedia of Islam*, s.v. "'Abd al-Malik"; Wellhausen, *The Arab Kingdom and its Fall*, pp. 188–216.

the outbreak of hostilities? If Theophanes should be correct, there was indeed another cause, one that has occasioned much scholarly disagreement, and if true, would reveal Justinian as a very foolish young man. This is the matter of the Arab coin reform.

It will be remembered that the caliph, by the terms of the treaty of 688, was obliged to pay a large tribute to the emperor. Until the reign of Abd-al-Malik, the Caliphate had not minted gold coins of its own, but rather used the gold bezants of the Empire. Consequently, the tribute to the Byzantine emperor was paid in Byzantine money. Then sometime in Abd-al-Malik's reign, the Arab government initiated the policy of minting its own gold pieces, stamped with the portrait of the caliph rather than the basileus. This change, according to Theophanes, offended Justinian highly; he stormily protested that he would not accept the payment in the "new" gold, and the next thing we know, the Arabs and the Byzantines were fighting it out over this matter.

Many scholars have accepted Theophanes' story as true, for after all, Abd-al-Malik was the initiator of the Arab coin reform. There are several points, however, which make it much more likely that the incident, while based on a core of historical fact, is largely legendary. The outstanding problem is one of the date; Abd-al-Malik's coinage reform is placed in the Arabic sources sometime after 692 (most probably 695).[8] There is, however, a counterargument here for those who trust Theophanes; perhaps the coins in question were experimental types minted by the Arabs before the initiation of the full-scale reform.[9] Specimens of such prereform types definitely exist. Yet they are very scarce and are mostly small denominations, apparently minted for local circulation and scarcely likely

[8] For details see James D. Breckenridge, *The Numismatic Iconography of Justinian II* (New York, 1959), pp. 71–73. Breckenridge heartily disbelieves Theophanes' story of the coin dispute.

[9] This is the point of view of Robert S. Lopez, "Mohammed and Charlemagne: A Revision," *Speculum* 18 (1943): 24. See also Philip Grierson, "The Monetary Reforms of Abd-al-Malik," *Journal of the Economic and Social History of the Orient* 3 (1960): 243.

to have been used in payment of the large Arab tribute to Byzantium. In sum, there do not seem to have been enough of the caliph's new coins available in 692 to have caused Justinian much anxiety.[10]

In addition to the matter of the date, the unlikeliness of Theophanes' story is enhanced by the fact that it was the Arabs who actually initiated hostilities against the Empire. If Justinian found the caliph's payment unacceptable and refused to receive it, it was hardly the Arabs' responsibility to force it on him, but rather his problem to make them pay it in the old style coinage.[11]

Nevertheless, Theophanes may at least preserve a grain of historical fact in suggesting that there was some disagreement over coins between the caliph and the basileus in 692. From the ninth-century Arab chronicler al-Balâdhuri come further insights into the whole picture. According to this Arab source, Abd-al-Malik's coin reform was preceded by the papyrus reform. Under the caliph's direction a new system was initiated of marking papyri for export to Byzantium with Moslem religious inscriptions. Ever since the Arab conquest of Egypt, the Byzantines had been dependent upon the Arabs for their papyrus supply. Naturally, the Christian Empire would not wish to use sheets of papyrus decorated with Moslem texts, and according to al-Balâdhuri's story, Justinian angrily threatened the caliph that unless the practice were stopped, he would place an inscription insulting Mohammed on the Empire's coinage.[12]

No such message ever appeared on Justinian II's coins, but at a point very close to the outbreak of the Arab-Byzantine war, the emperor did initiate a practice sure to be as offensive to a good Moslem as the papyrus reform was to him: for the first time in Byzantine history, the Empire minted coins stamped with an effigy of Christ (Figures 5 and 6). If there was squabbling over coins in 692, as Theophanes indicates, very likely it

[10] Breckenridge, *Numismatic Iconography*, p. 74.

[11] Ibid., p. 69.

[12] Al-Balâdhuri, cited by Wellhausen, *The Arab Kingdom and its Fall*, p. 217; see also Lopez, "Mohammed and Charlemagne," p. 24.

was the caliph protesting Justinian's coin reform rather than vice versa.[13] Later, after the brief war had run its course, the caliph would retaliate further against his Christian neighbor by full-scale abandonment of Byzantine coinage, replacing it with his own issues.

In any event, whatever the reasons, the fragile peace between Empire and Caliphate was broken as Arab forces came trooping across the Byzantine frontier in 692. With them they carried like a banner a copy of the broken treaty of 688, pierced full of holes and mounted on the point of a lance.[14] As we have seen, the ensuing battle of Sebastopolis was a disaster for the Byzantines. The emperor's Sklavinians deserted to the Arab side; they had, after all, no real reason to feel loyalty to the Empire, and probably the Arabs offered them better pay. Though the Arabs gained little if any territory as a result of their victory, Justinian II had suffered a grave setback, and the repercussions of Sebastopolis would haunt him throughout the remainder of his first reign. Following the Arab victory, an Armenian patrician, Symbatios (or Sembat) Bagratuni, led a revolt against Byzantine authority in that area and was instrumental in permitting the Arabs to regain a position in the southern part of Armenia.[15] Nor was this the only region where the Byzantines experienced Arab pressures. For the rest of Justinian's reign and throughout those of his immediate successors, Arab raiders continued to penetrate into Byzantine territory, rendering increasingly difficult the problem of the Empire's defense.

As for Cyprus, however, where much of the trouble originated in the first place, history has a somewhat happier note. Although the exact date is not known, the condominium arrangement was soon restored, and would continue to provide a basis for secure government on the island for many years longer,[16] while most of the Cypriot colonists who had

[13] Breckenridge, *Numismatic Iconography*, p. 75.

[14] Nikephoros, p. 37; Theophanes, p. 366.

[15] Theophanes, pp. 366–67; see also Grégoire, "An Armenian Dynasty on the Byzantine Throne," p. 18.

[16] Jenkins, "Cyprus between Byzantium and Islam," pp. 1013–14.

settled in Nea Justinianopolis were returned to their homeland by the Emperor Tiberius Apsimar in about 699.[17] Though the New City of Justinian was abandoned, it is interesting that the Metropolitan of Cyprus retained the title Archbishop of Nova Justiniana and all Cyprus,[18] and thus through the ages continued to bear witness to the name of the impetuous young emperor who touched upon the land's history in the first of its many centuries of Moslem-Christian unrest.

[17] Constantine VII, *De Administrando Imperio*, pp. 224–25. It is true that Constantine does not name the emperor who repatriated the Cypriots, but his information that the move took place "after seven years" makes it clear that it occurred in Apsimar's reign.

[18] Hackett, *History of the Orthodox Church of Cyprus*, pp. 44, 260–61; Hill, *History of Cyprus*, p. 290.

7

BUILDINGS AND COINS

I F JUSTINIAN'S military ventures were not uniformly successful, they proved at least something of the emperor's continued determination to get the better of his foes. Another side of the young sovereign's personality is revealed in his artistic sensibilities, particularly the extensive building program launched under his sponsorship. His interest in building was one of the ways in which Justinian most resembled his great predecessor whose name he bore. But while many of the first Justinian's projects, including the magnificent Hagia Sophia, have survived through the centuries to insure him undying fame as a patron of building, apparently nothing remains of the work sponsored by Justinian II. The frequent notices of his building program in our sources, however, show that in his own time and for many years thereafter, the second Justinian was remembered as a lavish builder.

Early in his reign, the young basileus undertook a series of additions to the Great Palace that far surpassed any similar accomplishments in the reigns of his immediate forebears. Unfortunately we have no concrete data concerning the artists and architects commissioned by the emperor, but clearly his interest in and lavish patronage of their creative projects rendered the court a center of revived artistic activity. Chief among the buildings erected under his sponsorship were two huge reception halls known as the *lausiacus* and the *triclinum*. The *lausiacus* seems to have served as a connection between the throne room and the section of the Great Palace known as the Daphne, while the *triclinum* provided an imperial passageway into the Hippodrome.[1] In the time of the Emperor Constantine VII, when these structures were still standing, the *triclinum* was generally called by palace dwellers "the Justinianos," in memory of its builder.[2]

In connection with Justinian's remodeling of the Great Palace, Theophanes presents an interesting anecdote, dating from late in Justinian's first reign.[3] According to this report, the emperor decided to build a fountain and a series of seats in a certain area of the palace complex where he might receive delegations from the deme of the Blues, one of the two political factions of early Byzantine history. This mention of the Blues is interesting in itself, for ordinarily Theophanes is very reluctant to mention either of the popular parties.[4] In any case, Justinian's project was complicated in this instance by the fact that a small chapel stood on the site where he wanted his fountain and reception area. The basileus, who attached great importance to outward signs of piety, realized that he could not have the chapel destroyed unless it was properly "deconsecrated." This led to considerable protest from the Patriarch of Constantinople, Kallinikos, whom Justinian asked to perform the deconsecration ceremony. But ultimately the patriarch yielded and pronounced a short, improvised prayer over the condemned chapel, reflecting clearly his disapproval of the whole matter: "Glory be to God, who is long-suffering now, always, and forever and ever. Amen!"

Among Justinian's plans for embellishment of his capital

[1] J. B. Bury, "The Great Palace," *Byzantinische Zeitschrift* 21 (1912): 219–21; see also Ostrogorsky, *History of the Byzantine State*, p. 140n1.

[2] Constantine VII Porphyrogenitus, *De Cerimoniis Aulae Byzantinae*, 1:286.

[3] Theophanes, p. 367. There is no corresponding notice in Nikephoros.

[4] The demes were far more active than either Theophanes or Nikephoros is willing to admit. See below, chapter 13. Incidentally, the fact that it was the Blues whom Justinian planned to receive in this particular area (although apparently he personally was a partisan of the Greens), indicates that he was not yet completely alienated from the deme that would play such a crucial role in his overthrow very shortly thereafter.

probably should also be included the set of six large golden plaques that decorated the Milion, the milestone in the center of the city from which all distances were measured. These plaques depicted the Six Ecumenical Councils and were one of the marvels of the capital until destroyed by the bitter iconoclast Constantine V. We have no specific information as to which emperor erected these memorials, but it must have been one in the late seventh or early eighth century, and Justinian II, whose reign is the longest of the emperors of this period and who was very interested in the accomplishments of the ecumenical councils, is by far the most likely possibility.[5]

Even though none of Justinian's construction projects have survived, we are able to obtain some further clues concerning the aesthetic sensitivities of the emperor from the coinage issued under his supervision. Numismatists have frequently commented on the fact that the coins of Justinian II are superior artistically to those of the other Heraclians. Apparently, some unknown die maker who was employed late in the reign of Constantine IV continued in the service of his son and was responsible for the prototypes of these designs.[6] Justinian II showed considerable originality in the designs he approved. His father Constantine IV was frequently pictured in military garb and in a pose deliberately copied from coins of his hero, Justinian I.[7] The second Justinian chose to imitate neither his father nor his great namesake, but to appear in civil costume. On a number of the issues of his first reign he is clothed in a *divitision* (tunic) and over it a *chlamys* (cloak). In harmony with the imperial fashion of several centuries, Justinian's *chlamys* is fastened on the right shoulder with an elaborate pin called the *fibula*, from which were suspended three jew-

[5] André Grabar, *L'Iconoclasme byzantin: dossier archéologique* (Paris, 1957), pp. 49, 55.

[6] Philip Grierson, *Catalogue of the Byzantine Coins in the Dumbarton Oaks Collection and in the Whittemore Collection*, 2 vols. to date (Washington, 1966–), 2:516.

[7] Alfred R. Bellinger, "The Gold Coins of Justinian II," *Archaeology* 8 (1950): 108.

elled pendants. His crown, surprisingly, is rather simple: a circlet topped by a cross.

On certain issues of his coinage, Justinian departed from the usual custom of showing only the emperor's head and shoulders, and introduced a full-length portrait of himself clad in the *loros* or ceremonial scarf and holding a large cross (Figure 5). Although the emperor's effigy on these issues is so small that it gives little hint as to his actual appearance, it is an attractive and distinctive design.

On some of Justinian's coins is imprinted his cipher, ✠, a pattern containing the letters of his name in Greek: I Ο Υ Ϲ Τ Ι Ν Ι Α Ν Ο Ϲ .[8] Practically every Byzantine emperor had such a cipher, and these designs were used widely. Not only were they imprinted on coins but they were stamped on bricks, carved into stone monuments, or woven into rich fabrics for imperial clothing. Justinian II's cipher, interestingly, is completely unlike that of Justinian I, though of course based upon the same letters.

By far the most original innovation in Justinian II's coinage is his introduction of the use of an effigy of Christ (Figure 6), a change which, as we have seen, may well have offended the caliph. The Christ figure used on the coins of Justinian's first reign is significant for other reasons also. It would have vast continuing influence in Christian art; most subsequent portrayals of Christ, not only in the Byzantine world but in western Christendom as well, would be derived directly or indirectly from the coinage of Justinian II.[9]

The use of the portrait of Christ on Justinian's money also necessitated moving the emperor's portrait to the reverse of the coin, for the first time in Byzantine history, though it is doubtful that Justinian's subjects paid as much attention to the distinction between obverse and reverse as modern numis-

---

[8] Grierson, *Dumbarton Oaks Catalogue*, 2:589, 590, etc.

[9] Breckenridge, *Numismatic Iconography*, p. 46; Ernst Kitzinger, "Some Reflections on Portraiture in Byzantine Art," *Vizantološkog instituta Zbornik radova* 8, no. 1 (1963): 191–92.

FIGURE 5
Justinian II in loros *(reverse of coin in Figure 6)*
Dumbarton Oaks Collection

matists do.[10] Probably more important in the Byzantine way of
thinking was the concept that Christ and the basileus appeared
together, on the two sides of one whole, typifying vividly the
earthly sovereign's role as deputy for the heavenly one. This
concept is further strengthened by the coin inscriptions.
Around the head of Christ appears the legend REX REGNANTIUM
(King of those who reign), while the emperor's portrait is
stamped with the phrase D. JUSTINIANUS SERVUS CHRISTI (Lord
Justinian, Slave of Christ). Never before had the epithet
Servus Christi been used to describe the emperor on Byzantine

---

[10] George P. Galavaris, "The Symbolism of the Imperial Costume as
Displayed on Byzantine Coins," *American Numismatic Society Museum
Notes* 8 (1958): 106–9.

FIGURE 6
*Image of Christ introduced on Justinian's
coinage c. 691/692*
Dumbarton Oaks Collection

coinage, although it is a phrase much in tune with the early
Christian way of thinking.[11] Some have suggested that Justinian in using this title was deliberately parodying the caliph,
whose name "Abd-al-Malik" literally means "slave of the
King."[12] While it is certainly not impossible that Justinian
realized the similarity here, it would be misleading to think it
his only reason for the choice. Coins served as a very valuable
means of getting imperial propaganda across to the people,
and here the message is basically one of the emperor as

[11] Breckenridge, *Numismatic Iconography*, pp. 63–67.
[12] Breckenridge, *Numismatic Iconography*, p. 66, discusses this theory
and finds it unacceptable.

Christ's deputy and as the upholder of orthodoxy. In it is an indication, which we see fulfilled in the unfolding of his religious policies, of Justinian's deep concern for the outward niceties of the faith. If from the modern point of view Justinian's religious sentiments seem incongruous with some of his more militant behavior, the world of his time would scarcely have seen it so. The concern he would display in his attempts to promote and strengthen the formal workings of the Christian Church within his empire was in all probability genuine. Here, indeed, more clearly than in any other area, Justinian II was a typical son of Byzantium.

8

JUSTINIAN,

CHAMPION OF ORTHODOXY

EVERY Byzantine emperor was expected to be vitally involved in religion. In the almost four centuries since the first Constantine converted to Christianity, the wearers of the Byzantine crown had included representatives of a wide assortment of religious views, from pagan to orthodox, with a liberal sprinkling of dedicated heretics. Diverse as the opinions of these imperial theologians might have been, there was scarcely an emperor who did not exhibit deep concern for religious matters. Justinian II was no exception; like his father before him, but unlike the earlier Heraclians, he chose the path of orthodoxy, a decision which caused him to take various actions against the most active groups of unorthodox Christians of his time, the Monotheletes and the Paulicians, and ironically would eventually lead him into a spectacular attempt to arrest the pope.

The Monothelete belief was a concoction of Justinian's great-great-grandfather, Heraclius of Carthage. Of course, Heraclius never intended to be heretical; he thought he was orthodox and that his suggestion that Jesus Christ possessed only a divine will and not a human one was a brilliant compromise that should end an earlier dispute, the Monophysite heresy. The Byzantines tended to involve themselves in theological definition with a fervor that utterly eludes most moderns. The "one will" concept evoked heated dispute, so intense that the Emperor Constans tried to end it by an imperial proclamation forbidding any further discussion of the question. This attempted moratorium on the controversy proved a dismal failure. Though Constans personally seems to have cared far less for theological subtleties than the typical Byzantine, he was enraged that his order to end the dispute was widely disregarded, and consequently undertook violent persecution of some of the leading spokesmen of the orthodox view. Still the dispute continued, and Justinian's father, Constantine IV, found it necessary to convoke the Sixth Ecumenical Council in 680. There, in what amounted to a reversal of the policy of the earlier Heraclians, orthodoxy was officially reestablished and the Monothelete belief officially denounced.

Early in Justinian II's first reign, either in 686 or the following year, he convoked a synod of bishops and other dignitaries to confirm the acts of his father's ecumenical council and thereby make clear his personal stand against Monotheletism.[1] Another probable reason for this meeting was to give the newly restored patriarch of Constantinople, Theodore, a repentant ex-Monothelete, a chance to acknowledge publicly his return to orthodoxy.[2] In a decree or *iussio* sent by Justinian to the pope informing him of the synod, we learn more of the young emperor's religious thinking at the time, and of another problem that led him to call the synod. Since this communique is one of the very few surviving documents actually issued by Justinian II, it is of particular interest. Significantly, there is in it no hint of Justinian's later troubles with the papacy. The emperor addresses the "universal Pope," "the most holy and blessed father" in a respectful though suitably imperial tone,

[1] The text of Justinian's report or *iussio* to the pope concerning this synod is printed in Mansi, *Concilia*, vol. 11, cols. 737–38. There is no precise information as to the date of the synod other than that it was held sometime before the *iussio* was issued, February 17, 687.

[2] So suggests Breckenridge, *Numismatic Iconography*, pp. 10–11. See also Augustin Fliche and Victor Martin, eds., *Histoire de l'Église*, vol. 5 (Paris, 1930), pp. 192–93, for a detailed treatment of the synod as a whole.

and his declared role as the champion of orthodoxy was such as was likely to win the pope's staunch approval.

Unfortunately, Justinian's *iussio* survives only in a very bad Latin translation. It is problematical whether the Latin version was produced by an imperial scribe in Constantinople or by someone at the papal court.[3] In any event, as clearly as can be made out, Justinian is expressing his dismay over the fact that one or more copies of the Acts (*gesta*) of the Sixth Council, most probably the originals, had been removed from their place in the palace without his imperial permission. These had been circulated to some unknown individuals who returned them to "certain of our judges." When he learned of this development, Justinian was surprised and clearly displeased, for he feared that forgers might have worked on the texts. He had not foreseen, he says, that anyone would remove the copies of the Acts without his permission, for he, the emperor, was the divinely appointed guardian of the "immaculate faith of Christ." Justinian's concern most likely was based on fear that the Acts had fallen or might fall into the hands of his opponents, the Monotheletes, who would alter them to suit their own beliefs. In order to assure a correct text, the emperor continues in his report to Rome, he had thus summoned the synod composed of various church and state officials. There the correct text of the Acts was publicly read and signed by the dignitaries present. Significantly, a papal *apocrisiarius* was among those participating in the meeting. The Acts were then entrusted to Justinian, who promised to preserve them "so that there will be no opportunity for those who do not wish to have fear of God to corrupt or change anything in them at any time it pleases them." Apparently Justinian had very little trouble from the Monotheletes during the rest of his first reign, and the heresy appeared to be gradually dying out.[4]

Although the news had not reached Constantinople, Pope

[3] For further detail see Franz Görres, "Justinian II und das römische Papsttum," *Byzantinische Zeitschrift* 17 (1908): 437. Görres supports the former alternative.

[4] Interestingly, however, it was a Monothelete, Philippikos Vardan, who eventually replaced Justinian as emperor. See below, chapter 21.

John V, to whom Justinian addressed his communication on the synod, had died in August, 686, a full half-year before the *iussio* was written. This is a vivid example of the slowness of communication between Rome and Constantinople in this era, a problem which rendered effective working relations between pope and emperor difficult even at best. When the *iussio* finally reached Rome, it was received by the new pope, Conon. The *Liber Pontificalis* (*Book of the Popes*, written contemporaneously with the events it described) records the arrival of Justinian's decree in favorable terms.[5] There is certainly no indication that the Roman church viewed Justinian's promise "to guard and preserve forever unimpaired and unshaken" the Acts of the Sixth Council as any infringement on papal prerogatives[6]; rather, the young emperor was manifesting encouraging signs of following his father's role as a defender of orthodoxy.

Pope Conon had further reason to be pleased when two other imperial rescripts arrived, also in 687.[7] In one, Justinian reduced taxes on certain papal territories: to be specific, he remitted two hundred measures of the annual tax (*annonae*) levied upon the patrimony of Bruttium and Lucania. In the other rescript, he did another favor for the pope by directing that a number of papal peasants who were being held in pledge by the militia be restored to Bruttium and Lucania and to Sicily. There is no precise hint as to what prompted Justinian to these acts of good will, but somewhat similar remissions of taxes had been granted previously by Constantine IV, thanks to the intervention of papal officials in Constantinople.[8]

[5] *Liber Pontificalis*, 1:368.

[6] Görres, "Justinian II und das römische Papsttum," pp. 439–40, however, takes the view that this early synod of Justinian's was a reversal of his father's policy of good will toward the papacy and a foretaste of his more determined efforts at papal control manifested in the aftermath of the Quinisext Council.

[7] The original texts are not preserved; summaries of their content are in *Liber Pontificalis*, 1:369. For the significance of these rescripts from the standpoint of Justinian's reputed tax reform, see below, chapter 12.

[8] For details see Horace K. Mann, *The Lives of the Popes in the Early Middle Ages*, 2d ed., vol. 1, pt. 2 (London, 1925), p. 46.

Probably something similar had occurred in this case. Pope Conon thus had a number of reasons to be pleased with Justinian II, and scarcely could have guessed that within a few years his successor, Sergius I, would experience grave difficulties with the same emperor.

Before proceeding further with the subject of imperial-papal relations, some notice should be made of another indication of orthodoxy manifested by the young basileus. Sometime during his first reign, about 690 or perhaps earlier, Justinian received a report from the bishop of Koloneia concerning activities of the dualistic sect of the Paulicians of Armenia.[9] Constantine IV had earlier taken steps to suppress this new variety of heresy, and now that Paulician teaching was spreading again, Justinian ordered an investigation. A wave of persecution followed, and death by fire was decreed for those who obstinately refused to give up their views and to profess orthodox Christianity. Among the Paulicians executed was their leader, Symeon-Titus.[10] It must be remembered that in an era when suppression of heresy was deemed a virtue and religious tolerance was not, this anti-Paulician effort of Justinian II would be reckoned by most of his contemporaries as one of his positive accomplishments. It is notable, therefore, that there is no mention of it in the chronicles of either Nikephoros or Theophanes. Perhaps we have here an instance where anti-Justinian propagandists have suppressed an item that would appear too much to the fallen emperor's credit, though it is

[9] On the history and beliefs of the Paulicians, the most comprehensive work is Nina G. Garsoïan, *The Paulician Heresy* (The Hague, 1967). The only primary source for imperial persecution of the Paulicians this early in their history is a work generally attributed to Petrus Siculus, *Historia Manichaeorum*, J.-P. Migne, ed., Patrologiae Cursus Completus: Series Graeca, vol. 104 (Paris, 1896). Justinian is called in this text "Justin reigning after Heraclius," but it is clear from the context that Justinian II is meant. Garsoïan, pp. 55–64, shows that Petrus's work is in all probability a composite of earlier sources.

[10] Petrus Siculus, *Historia Manichaeorum*, cols. 1281–82. See also Garsoïan, *Paulician Heresy*, pp. 117–18; Steven Runciman, *The Medieval Manichee* (Cambridge, 1947), pp. 35–38.

equally possible that the Paulicians were as yet simply too obscure to attract the chroniclers' notice.

In any event, it is clear that in his dealings with both Monotheletes and Paulicians, Justinian II was determined to be a rigorous upholder of orthodoxy. Further evidence of his enthusiastic involvement in religious issues was yet to come with his Quinisext Council, a convocation that was destined to become one of his pet projects, and yet, for all the professed good intentions behind it, was to lead him into numerous difficulties.

9

THE CANONS OF THE
QUINISEXT COUNCIL

Justinian's council, the Quinisext or Penthecton, was from its inception designed to be a continuation of both the Fifth and the Sixth Ecumenical Councils. Undoubtedly in his insistence upon this point, the emperor had in mind the fact that the Fifth Council, held in 553, had been the work of Justinian I, while the much more recent Sixth Council was an accomplishment of Constantine IV. In calling his own gathering the Quinisext, or Fifth-Sixth, Justinian II could thus picture himself as continuator of the work not only of his father but also of the emperor for whom he was named and to whose memory he was so conscientiously attached. Because neither the Fifth nor the Sixth Councils had issued any disciplinary canons but had confined their work strictly to the area of doctrine, Justinian's objective for his Quinisext was to fill this gap. Thus, the fathers who convened in the Domed Hall of the imperial palace under his sponsorship would not deal with theological problems in the strict sense of the term, but rather would confine their efforts to promulgation of a set of one hundred and two canons designed to upgrade the moral standards and practices of orthodox Christians, both clergy and laity.[1]

[1] The full text of the canons in the original Greek and in Latin translation is printed in Mansi, *Concilia*, vol. 11, cols. 921–1006. There is an

There has been much scholarly confusion on the date of
the convocation of the Quinisext, a problem that stems in part
from the fact that the Byzantine New Year was September 1
and that their general practice of numbering years was by the
fifteen-year indiction cycle. It is now usually accepted that the
council convened sometime in the year beginning September
1, 691.[2] Because the meetings were held in the Domed (Trullan) Hall of the palace, the Quinisext is occasionally referred
to as the Trullan Council or the Council in Trullo.

Dealing as they do with a wide variety of abuses, the
canons of the Quinisext provide many vivid glimpses into the
social history of the time. Although the rulings were not
arranged in any strictly logical order, certain themes stand
out as major concerns: uprooting of surviving pagan customs,
much specific attention to marriage and celibacy laws, the
attempt to secure empire-wide conformity in a number of
liturgical and worship practices, and strict insistence on higher
standards of moral conduct. In the opening address of the
council to the emperor, the speaker sounds a note recurring
in the appeals of would-be reformers throughout history: the
present age is an era of moral decay; the Church is not what
it used to be. Nevertheless, the speaker continued, in typical
terms of imperial flattery, Christians could rejoice, for God
had sent his people a protector, Justinian.[3] One may imagine
the twenty-two-year-old emperor listening to these words with
glowing satisfaction and picturing how he would go down in
the annals of Christian history along with Constantine IV, Justinian I, and the other great emperors of the past whom the

---

English translation with lengthy commentary in Philip Schaff and Henry
Wace, eds., A Select Library of the Nicene and Post Nicene Fathers, 2d
series, vol. 14 (New York, 1900), pp. 356–408. Also very useful are Hefele,
History of the Councils, 5:221–42, and Fliche and Martin, Histoire de
l'Église, 5:194–97.

[2] Additional confusion arose from a copyist's mistake in the citation
of the annus mundi in an early manuscript of the canons. For details see
Hefele, Councils, 5:222–23.

[3] Mansi Concilia, vol. 11, cols. 921–30.

Church still venerated for their participation in the ecumenical councils.

It is not clear whether Justinian II was present for all the sessions of the Quinisext, but his attendance certainly would not have been at all unusual. The canons promulgated were matters which undoubtedly met with his hearty approval, and which show thereby some of the practices of the time that seemed to him and to the council fathers to stand in need of correction.

Among the most interesting canons for insight into the life of the people are those which deal with survivals of ancient Greek paganism. A number of heathen festivals were still being celebrated in Christian Byzantium, including the *Bota* in honor of Pan, the *Brumalia* in honor of Bacchus, and a great holiday on March 1, the ancient Roman New Year. The Quinisext fathers ruled that such celebrations must stop. Public dances in honor of the old gods, especially those in which men dressed as women and women as men, were likewise forbidden, as was the wearing of masks—comic, tragic, and satyric—remnants of the old Greek theater now considered to have pagan overtones. The custom of invoking the ancient wine-god, Bacchus, even in jest, during the production of wine was an additional sign of pagan "insanity" frowned upon by the council fathers. Persons who transgressed in regard to any of these stipulations were to be excommunicated if laymen, and if churchmen, deposed from their clerical status (canon 62). In another canon (65), the same penalties are decreed for those who practiced the old pagan custom of building a bonfire and leaping over it. Such fires, it seems, were regularly lit in front of homes and shops to celebrate the new moon and often became the occasion for drunken carousing.

Further injunctions against pagan practices occur in other pronouncements of the Quinisext; in one (canon 94), excommunication is prescribed for anyone who swears any kind of heathen oath. Students of civil law received a special warning against pagan customs in canon 71, a pronouncement which in its concern about student behavior has a strangely timeless tone. Students were "not to wear clothing contrary to the general custom," the council fathers warned, nor to waste time at theatrical or athletic events.

In another attack on paganistic survivals (canon 61), the men of the council placed a stern prohibition on fortune-telling, casting of horoscopes, selling of bear's hair and other magical amulets, and similar superstitious practices. Those who transgressed against any of these injunctions were to be required to do six years penance. This canon was probably widely ignored, for the Byzantines tended to possess an inordinate interest in foretelling the future. A few years later, Justinian himself would be listening hopefully to the glowing predictions of a certain monk named Cyrus, probably without a thought that he was violating one of his own canons.

Along with their campaign against pagan practices, the members of the Quinisext Council also possessed determination to "protect" Christians from possible influences of Judaism. Anti-Semitism was rife in the Christian empire, and hence it is no surprise to find the council stipulating excommunication for laymen and deposition for clerics who eat Jewish unleavened bread, receive medicine from Jews, bathe with them, or otherwise have confidential dealings with them (canon 11).

A number of canons (87, 98, 91, 92, 86, 100) are specifically concerned with improving the moral standards and conduct of both clergy and laity. There are a number of injunctions, some of them simply restatements of the work of earlier councils, against such serious matters as adultery, abortion, rape, brothel-keeping, and pornography. The Quinisext fathers took note, too, of numerous lesser transgressions. For instance, no one was to cut up and put to profane use old copies of the Bible or the writings of the Church Fathers unless such books were completely worn out, "rendered useless either by bookworms or by water or in some other way" (canon 68). Singing in church was not to be done in a loud or rowdy manner; one must not "force nature to shouting" (canon 75). Persons were not to eat in church or sell food there (canon 76). Animals were not to be brought inside a church building except in a real emergency, such as taking shelter from a storm (canon 88). Wigs and false hairpieces, which apparently were worn not only by women but also by men, even clerics, were condemned; one should "adorn the inner man rather than the outer," the council fathers admonished (canon 96).

In many of the canons, particular emphasis was placed on high standards for the clergy. Clerics were forbidden to take interest on loans, to work as tavern keepers, and to take part in horse races (canons 10, 9, 24). When present at a wedding festival, persons in religious orders were to leave before the celebration of games began (canon 24). Clerics and laymen alike were forbidden to play dice or to participate as actors, dancers, or animal-fighters in theatrical shows, with the usual penalty stipulated of excommunication for lay offenders, deposition for clerics (canons 50, 51). It is doubtful how effective these stringent curbs on theatrical performances could have been in a city so noted for its love of spectacular entertainments as Constantinople was. Attempts to enforce the new restrictions might well have been one of the causes for Justinian's sinking popularity with the people of his capital.

Clarification of various marriage and celibacy rules formed another major theme in the work of the Quinisext.[4] There were also a number of canons dealing with liturgical practices and the condemnation of local customs out of harmony with the practices of the ecumenical church. The fathers of the Quinisext were particularly worried about certain peculiar practices of the Armenians and of the "barbarians" of the West, and singled these out for special attention. There are four canons (32, 33, 56, 99) forbidding the Armenian practices of offering communion wine unmixed with water, of ordaining to the priesthood only members of certain priestly families, of eating eggs and cheese on Saturdays and Sundays in Lent, and of cooking meat to serve to priests inside of the church

---

[4] In canons 3–6, 12–13, 26, 30, 44, 47–48, 53–54, 87, 93, and 98.

sanctuary. Undoubtedly there was objection to these new rulings when they were announced in Armenia, although a number of Armenian bishops were present at the Quinisext and their subscriptions to the canons indicate that they were convinced the reform should be attempted. Still it seems likely that the unrest in Armenia shortly thereafter and Byzantine losses to the Arabs in this area were tied in with popular resistance to the proposed changes.

In the West, the lands so undiplomatically described as "barbarian," Justinian's Quinisext canons would encounter even stronger opposition, from none other than the pope himself. The emperor's struggle with Pope Sergius deserves detailed consideration, but before turning to this heated dispute, it is important to notice that in spite of Western opposition, the Eastern church from the outset accepted Justinian's council as ecumenical and its canons as valid and binding.[5] In light of this fact, the omission of any mention of the council by the Patriarch Nikephoros and only a confused, brief statement about it by the monk Theophanes[6] are striking indeed. A possible explanation is that the "713 Chronicle" used by Nikephoros was already so biased against Justinian that it was deemed necessary to omit any mention of his role in sponsoring the Quinisext Council; to do so would be to connect him too closely with an action of which the Church approved. Theophanes had access to fuller information, yet his vagueness indicates that the unwillingness of Byzantine historians to associate Justinian II with the council must have continued even as the trend to depict the emperor generally in most unfavorable terms persisted and grew during the eighth century.

There is on the other hand one strange and notable exception to the usual depreciation of Justinian in Byzantine

[5] Hefele, *Councils*, 5:221; Schaff and Wace, *Post Nicene Fathers*, 14:356–58.

[6] Theophanes, pp. 361–62, quotes in detail from canon 3 on clerical marriages, which indicates that he had access to a copy of the canons. He says almost nothing, however, about the council's other activities, is confused as to the date, and records nothing of the emperor's subsequent struggle with the papacy.

historiography: the fact that some Eastern Orthodox saint calendars used to include him as St. Justinian Rhinotmetos. His feast day was July 15. His major claim to sainthood must have been his sponsorship of the Quinisext, for it was fairly standard procedure in the Orthodox Church to reckon among the saints the deceased emperors who had been associated with the ecumenical councils. In modern times, no doubt because the chroniclers' evaluation of Justinian's misrule came to be almost universally believed, his name has been expunged from the Orthodox calendar.[7] Even so, the fact that Justinian was ever considered saintly may indicate that in bygone centuries there existed traditions about him far different from those recorded by his historiographical adversaries, Nikephoros and Theophanes.

[7] F. G. Holweck, *A Biographical Dictionary of the Saints* (St. Louis, 1924), p. 577. See also Adrian Fortescue, *The Orthodox Eastern Church* (London, n.d.), p. 104.

10

POPE SERGIUS PROTESTS

JUSTINIAN II does not seem to have anticipated the papacy's forthcoming resistance to the canons of the Quinisext. At the concluding session of the council, the emperor signed his name in the red ink traditionally used for imperial signatures on each of six copies of the canons.[1] A space was left immediately after Justinian's name for the signature of the pope. Then followed the ratification of the canons by the four patriarchs of the East, of Constantinople, Alexandria, Jerusalem, and Antioch. John, the Archbishop of Nea Justinianopolis, was accorded the privilege of signing immediately after the patriarchs,[2] and after him, the more than two hundred bishops and their representatives who had attended the council affixed their signatures to the canons. The "Tomes," all six copies, were then forwarded to Rome for ratification by Pope Sergius I.

Sergius, who was destined to prove such a staunch foe of the canons, had been pope since 687. He was by birth a Syrian, but had grown up in Palermo, Sicily. From the *Liber*

---

[1] That the emperor's signature was in red is specifically mentioned in a note on the manuscript of the copy of the canons from which Mansi's printed text was derived. The six copies of the canons were designated for eventual possession of the emperor, the pope, and the four patriarchs. Duchesne, *Liber Pontificalis*, 1:378n.

[2] An additional indication of Justinian's favoritism for his colony of transplanted Cypriots.

Pontificalis, which is full of interesting small details, we learn that he was especially talented in music; it was his childhood participation as a choirboy that had eventually led him into the religious vocation.[3]

As pope, Sergius seems to have been dynamic and popular with the Roman people. Their support for him in the forthcoming crisis is clearly indicative of how tenuous was the hold of the Byzantine Empire in Italy, and how in cases of conflict of loyalties the Italians, though Byzantine subjects, often tended to feel stronger allegiance to the pope than to the emperor.

When Sergius received and read the Tomes, he not only refused to sign them, he also prohibited any public reading of them. "I would rather be dead," he reputedly exclaimed, "than to consent to the new errors they contain!"[4] At this point the question naturally arises as to what material in the canons so offended the pope. Various historians in subsequent times have emphasized diverse reasons why the Quinisext Council was unacceptable to Rome.[5] Any or all of these factors may well have influenced Sergius to take the stand he did.

First of all, the question arises of whether or not the pope had had any official representatives at the Quinisext. If he did not, this would of course be a most valid cause for complaint. Yet according to the author of the *Liber Pontificalis*, who would have been in a position to know, papal legates had actually been present in Constantinople and signed the canons there, although, the papal chronicler adds, they did not understand what they signed.[6] So far the matter seems clear enough. There is some question, however, as to the status of these legates: were they sent to Constantinople especially to take part

[3] *Liber Pontificalis*, 1:372.

[4] Ibid., 373.

[5] Important secondary source treatments of Justinian's controversy with Pope Sergius include Görres, "Justinian II und das römische Papsttum," pp. 440–51; Fliche and Martin, *Histoire de l'Église*, 5:195–97; Hefele, *Councils*, 5:237–40; Mann, *Lives of the Popes*, vol. 1, pt. 2, pp. 87–92.

[6] *Liber Pontificalis*, 1:372.

in the Quinisext or were they permanent resident representatives of the pope in the Byzantine capital? The *Liber Pontificalis* does not say, but it seems likely that the latter explanation is the correct one.[7]

A further question arises as to what it was they actually signed, for the names of the legates do not appear on the official list of signers of the Tomes. Probably they consented to some earlier version of the council's proceedings. They would not be included in the final list of signers, since it was composed almost altogether of bishops. There were only a few exceptions where some deacon had been specifically deputed to sign on his bishop's behalf. Since the men of the council had anticipated that Sergius would ratify the canons personally and since the pope's personal signature would carry much more weight than that of a mere deputy, it must have seemed that there was no need for his legates to sign the final copies for him.

The reason why the legates indicated consent to the canons at all is also problematical. The *Liber Pontificalis* says merely that they were "deceived" as to the true meaning of the offensive canons. Perhaps they did not dare to oppose the emperor's wishes, or perhaps they simply had no idea how vigorously Pope Sergius would react against the work of the Quinisext. In any event, Sergius could take comfort in the fact that their names were not on the final copies of the Tomes.

There was, however, one signature on the Tomes that must have worried Sergius considerably, although the *Liber Pontificalis* does not mention it. This is the subscription of Archbishop Basil of Gortyna in Crete, who added after his name the cryptic phrase "holding the place of all the Synod of the holy Church of Rome."[8] In 680, this Basil had been commissioned by the Roman Synod to be its representative at the Sixth Ecumenical Council and it seems that he arbitrarily

[7] Hefele, *Councils,* 5:238; Mann, *Lives of the Popes,* vol. 1, pt. 2, p. 90.

[8] Mansi, *Concilia,* vol. 11, col. 990.

reassigned himself to this position at the Quinisext.[9] Apparently, Pope Sergius thought the best thing to do about Basil's signature was to ignore it.

Still, the fact that Basil and also the legates were present at the Quinisext proceedings clearly indicates that Rome was not being deliberately excluded from taking part in the council, as some scholars have asserted. East-West communication, hindered as it was by Arab pirates in the Mediterranean and semibarbaric Sklavinians and Bulgars in the Balkans, was hazardous at best. It is true that the West lacked extensive representation at the Quinisext, but this is probably much more validly explained by the difficulty of travel than by the assumption of antipapal feelings on the part of Justinian II. Moreover, the overwhelming predominance of Eastern churchmen at Justinian's council was by no means an innovation of the Quinisext. The trend was already apparent in earlier ecumenical councils, increasing with the breakdown of East-West communication.

Nevertheless, the apparent lack of sufficient regard for the West would not incline Pope Sergius to a warm reception of the Tomes. Much more serious in the pope's eyes, however, was the fact that a few canons were in actual opposition to Roman practice, and it was probably more for this reason than for any question of representation that he was motivated to take a vigorous stand against the proceedings of the Quinisext as a whole. On the surface, canon 36 appears one of the most likely to be offensive to the papacy, for it states that the Patriarchate of Constantinople should enjoy the same rights as that of Rome, be as highly regarded in ecclesiastical matters, and rank second only to Rome in the hierarchy of bishoprics (that is, before the "apostolic" patriarchates of Alexandria, Antioch, and Jerusalem). But since canon 36 is basically a restatement of decrees promulgated by both the Second and the Fourth Ecumenical Councils, and as such already approved by the

---

[9] For further detail see Hefele, *Councils*, 5:238, which points out that Crete did belong to the patriarchate of Rome and that it is not impossible that Sergius actually gave him a specific deputation to attend the Quinisext.

papacy, the Roman pontiff actually had small ground for valid complaint on this issue.[10]

The marriage rules for the lower orders of clergy set forth in canon 13 definitely run counter to Western practices. According to this enactment, a married man who desired ordination as deacon or presbyter could be so ordained. He was then to be permitted, indeed required, to continue to live with his wife, and if he sent her away, was to be excommunicated. The Roman practice, conversely, required the vow of celibacy from any man ordained as deacon or presbyter; if married, he and his wife had to agree to permanent separation. As the framers of the Quinisext canons pointed out, the Roman custom was in clear opposition to what they called "apostolic canon" 6, which in theory the Roman church accepted. Nevertheless, the men of the council must have foreseen the difficulty that an attempt to change the status quo would cause in the Western church, for in canon 30 they provided a loophole permitting clerics "in the lands of the barbarians" to retain their own previous practices. There is indeed a patronizing tone in this canon's reference to the "smallness of soul and strangeness and lack of steadfastness of customs" of the Western clergy, but in spite of this, the enactment provides a definite overture to compromise, and may even reflect the influence of the papal legates at the council. On the other hand, its inference of Western inferiority may have been the item most offensive to the pope.[11]

A few other Western customs were flatly rejected by the Quinisext with no qualifications. The eighty-five "apostolic canons," of which the Western church recognized only the first fifty, were reconfirmed in Quinisext canon 2. Fasting on Saturdays in Lent, a popular Roman practice, was forbidden (canon 55). Abstinence from blood and the meat of strangled

[10] Ibid. On the other hand Görres, "Justinian II und das römische Papsttum," p. 444, views canon 36 as a "formal declaration of war" against the papacy and probably the item that offended Sergius most.

[11] For more detail on the differences on clerical marriages see Fliche and Martin, Histoire de l'Église, 5:196; Schaff and Wace, Post Nicene Fathers, 14:365–68.

animals was required on the basis of a biblical injunction which the West disregarded (canon 67).[12] Artistic representation of Christ as a lamb was prohibited; he was to be depicted only in human form (canon 82). This ruling against representation of Christ as the "Lamb of God" is of particular interest to historians of Byzantine art. Together with another of the Quinisext canons (73) forbidding the use of a cross in designs for floors,[13] it is the most significant instance of imperial concern for the proper use of icons in the pre-iconoclastic era.[14] Like all the Heraclian dynasty, Justinian II apparently attached great importance to the matter of icon veneration, and he seems to have been concerned lest some of his ignorant subjects actually think Christ appeared in the form of a lamb. It is tempting to see at this point a direct connection between the Quinisext Council and the Christ image that appeared on Justinian's coins for the first time at along about this time, but concrete evidence is lacking.[15]

On the other hand, Pope Sergius must have taken special notice of the ban on the "Lamb of God" image, since he possessed a special preference for this biblical metaphor that the council so condemned. It was in fact Sergius who added the singing of the "Agnus Dei" to the celebration of the Mass.[16]

In any case, whatever objections weighed most heavily in his mind, Pope Sergius made it absolutely clear that he would not sign the Tomes. Negotiations on the matter continued to drag on for many months, and neither Justinian nor Sergius showed any inclination to yield. At length, the emperor sent to

[12] Cf. Acts 15:29. The Western church viewed this requirement as a temporary measure of apostolic times aimed at promoting harmony between Jewish and gentile converts to Christianity. Hefele, *Councils,* 5:232n3.

[13] This was a reenactment of an earlier requirement of Theodosius II. Breckenridge, *Numismatic Iconography,* p. 82.

[14] Ernst Kitzinger, "The Cult of Images in the Age before Iconoclasm,"*Dumbarton Oaks Papers* 8 (1954): 120; Grabar, *L'Iconoclasme byzantin,* p. 80.

[15] Breckenridge, *Numismatic Iconography,* pp. 83–86, discusses the matter in detail. See also Grabar, *L'Iconoclasme byzantin,* p. 36.

[16] *Liber Pontificalis,* 1:372.

Rome a special envoy called a *magisterianus* who arrested and brought back to Constantinople two papal supporters, John, Bishop of Portus, and Boniface, "a councilor of the apostolic see."[17] Still Pope Sergius remained adamant.

How was an emperor to deal with such an uncooperative pope? Justinian II could find in the pages of his empire's history more than one helpful suggestion. His own grandfather, the Emperor Constans, had had Pope Martin I arrested, imprisoned, and subjected to extremely harsh treatment until Martin eventually died, probably of starvation, an exile in Cherson. There was also the example of the first Justinian, who had brought Pope Vigilius to Constantinople as an unwilling guest. Perhaps with these precedents in mind, Justinian II decided that Pope Sergius must be arrested, and thus he dispatched Zacharias the *protospatharius*, an officer of the imperial bodyguard, to Italy. His orders were to return to Constantinople bringing the pope.[18]

Justinian's plan failed to account for popular loyalty to the papacy. As the rumor of Sergius's pending fate spread through Italy, many men from the local militia of Ravenna, Ancona, and the surrounding area took up the pope's cause and marched on Rome to protect him.[19] Zacharias had already reached Rome by this time; the Byzantine officer now commanded that the city gates be locked, and personally took refuge in the papal palace, "shaking and asking tearfully that the pope have mercy on him." Along about this time the militia stormed through one of the city gates. Accompanied by a mob of the local citizenry, they headed straight for Sergius's residence, and while they stood outside shouting, the terrified Zacharias hid himself under the pope's bed. There he seemed

[17] Ibid., 373.

[18] The information on the Zacharias incident is derived from *Liber Pontificalis*, 1:373–74.

[19] It is perhaps significant that the author of the *Liber Pontificalis* does not mention the *exercitus Romanus*, the local Roman militia, among the pope's adherents. This would indicate that they, at least, remained technically loyal to the emperor, yet they do not seem to have made any effort to oppose Sergius's rescuers. Duchesne, *Liber Pontificalis*, 1:378n.

likely to remain until Sergius agreed to intercede on his behalf with the crowd outside the palace. The pontiff's defenders, moved by his appeal, agreed to spare Zacharias's life on the condition that he should withdraw immediately. Thus the Byzantine officer emerged from hiding to be driven out of Rome "with injuries and insults" and to face the dismal prospect of returning to Justinian with the report of his failure.

As events turned out, Zacharias was spared the interview with his emperor, for very soon after the trouble in Rome there broke out in Constantinople the revolt of Leontios that was to cost Justinian his nose and his throne. The troublesome Tomes of the Quinisext seemed permanently shelved as far as the papacy was concerned, though ten years later when Justinian returned to power, Rome was again to feel the force of his strong will.

11

SOLDIERS AND FARMERS

BEFORE we examine the matter of how Justinian came to suffer *rhinokopia* and lose his empire, there remain a number of routine administrative matters connected with his first reign that deserve notice. As we have seen, one theme that recurs with great frequency is his establishment of military colonies and resettlement of large groups of people, such as the Mardaïtes, Sklavinians, and Cypriots, in new locations far from their homelands. These moves are representative of his larger policy of placing people where they would be of most value to the Empire's defenses. Justinian II was by no means the first emperor to undertake such population shifting, nor would he be the last, but it seems clear that he did it with as much vigor as any Byzantine sovereign ever possessed in the whole matter of relocation. It seems clear, too, that while some of his colonization programs failed, the picture as a whole is one of long-range success.[1]

Justinian's colonization program is but one aspect of the large question of Byzantine provincial administration in this period. At the outset, it must be noted that modern Byzantine scholars are still sharply divided on several points in the administrative development of the seventh- and eighth-century Empire. Many changes took place at this time: changes in the

[1] For further details see especially Charanis, "The Transfer of Population as a Policy in the Byzantine Empire," pp. 140–43; Ostrogorsky, *History of the Byzantine State*, pp. 130 ff.

governmental machinery of the provinces, changes in the status of the peasantry, and in the laws and customs of landholding. It is not clear at every turn whether these innovations were programs closely worked out by and attributable to specific emperors or whether they were developments that simply occurred gradually without a definite long-range plan. In any case, Justinian II lived and ruled during part of the time when such changes were occurring rapidly, and there are several strong indications that he usually favored them.

There is scarcely any question in Byzantine history more hotly debated by modern scholars than that of the origins of the themes or military provinces so characteristic of the middle centuries of the Byzantine epoch.[2] The chroniclers are of very little help on such matters. They wrote of great events, of wars and revolutions, of the succession of the emperors and the fortunes of the dynasties. For day-to-day routine matters, they said very little. Thus, modern scholars cannot say with absolute certainty when the Byzantine state first decided to abandon the old Roman system of separation of military and civil authority in certain provinces and undertook the formation of units called themes, each headed by a strategos, who was both civil governor and commander-in-chief of the military forces stationed in the area. Some features of the thematic system certainly reach back before the time of Heraclius, while its full-blown development probably should not be dated until somewhat later than his reign.[3] Leaving aside many complex arguments on this issue, it is safe to generalize that the thematic system evolved under the Heraclian dynasty. We know, too, that thematic organization worked well in the perennial crisis situation of the seventh century and played a

[2] Of great importance is the study of Walter E. Kaegi, "Some Reconsiderations on the Themes," *Jahrbuch des Osterreichischen Gesellschaft* 16 (1967): 39–54, which presents an excellent summary of recent scholarly work in this area.

[3] Kaegi, "Reconsiderations," p. 39, summarizes the growing scholarly consensus on this point. Also important is Peter Charanis, "Some Remarks on the Changes in Byzantium in the Seventh Century," *Vizantološkog instituta Zbornik radova* 8, no. 1 (1963): 74–75.

vital role in preserving the Empire from total absorption by the Arabs and the barbarians.

Like his predecessors, Justinian II was concerned with maintaining and extending the themes. From early in his reign (February, 687) comes a document—his report to the pope on confirmation of the Acts of the Sixth Council—which has excited much interest among scholars of Byzantine administration, for in it Justinian included a list of the themes in organized operation at that time.[4] It might seem that such a list would be simple enough to decipher, but because of strange spelling and geographic uncertainties there has been considerable dispute as to precisely what areas the emperor was naming at one or two points. According to most scholars, there are five definitely established themes on Justinian's list.[5] These included, in Asia Minor, the Opsikion, Anatolikon, and Armeniakon themes about which there is little dispute. More uncertainty is involved in Justinian's mention of the theme of the Thracians: was it also in Asia Minor or is it to be identified with Thrace on the European side of the Bosphoros? The latter alternative is probably the correct one, although there is scholarly support for either view.[6] Even more problematical is Justinian's reference to the *Cabarisiani*. Many scholars have seen this as a reference to the maritime theme of the Caravisiani, but this identification has been questioned.[7]

There is no such problem when Justinian also mentions on his list the exarchates of Italy (Ravenna) and Africa (Carthage) on the more distant frontiers of the Empire. Each of these areas was administered by an exarch whose role as both military and civil governor was similar to that of a strategos.

From the same imperial document that contains the list of

[4] Mansi, *Concilia*, vol. 11, cols. 737–38.

[5] For example, Ostrogorsky, *History of the Byzantine State*, p. 132.

[6] Charles Diehl, "L'Origine du régime des thèmes dans l'empire byzantin," *Études byzantines* (Paris, 1905), p. 283; Hélène Antoniadis-Bibicou, *Études d'histoire maritime de Byzance* (Paris, 1966), pp. 68 ff.

[7] For details see Diehl, "L'Origine du régime des thèmes," p. 285, and more recently Antoniadis-Bibicou, *Études d'histoire maritime*, pp. 63–68.

themes comes the further significant notice that it was apparently customary that the exarchs and strategoi be represented at important meetings of the imperial council. The particular session that Justinian is describing in his report to the pope was held in order to reconfirm the Acts of the Sixth Ecumenical Council, but this instance could well be typical of the usual practice. What voice the provincial authorities had in actual policy-making is more uncertain, but at least their presence indicates something of the form of imperial council meetings at the time.

During the course of Justinian's first reign, at least one additional theme was founded. The first datable mention of the theme of Hellas (in central Greece) is in 695 with the appointment of Leontios (soon to be Justinian's successor) as strategos. It seems probable, however, that Hellas was organized as a theme a few years earlier, just after Justinian's victorious campaign against the Sklavinians of the Balkans,[8] and that it was designed to provide defense against further Sklavinian inroads into central Greece.

Closely related to the development of the theme system is another much-debated question of Byzantine military policy: the granting of land to soldiers in payment for their military service. According to many distinguished scholars, the men who made up the armies of the themes were also farmers, free, independent small landowners, cultivating their fields in peacetime and fighting the more zealously to defend them in times of invasion.[9] If this theory is a correct understanding, these military freeholders would be one of the most vital factors in maintaining the Empire's strength. Among the latest trends, however, in modern Byzantine scholarship are the stern warnings of several outstanding authorities that the older interpretation of farmers as soldiers is much overdrawn. While many Byzantine enlisted men undoubtedly came from

[8] Vasiliev, "L'Entrée triomphale de l'empereur Justinien II," p. 367.

[9] This interpretation is most associated with Ostrogorsky and is set forth in his *History of the Byzantine State*, pp. 132–37, and in a number of his monographs, for example, "Byzantine Cities in the Early Middle Ages," *Dumbarton Oaks Papers* 13 (1959): 45–47.

rustic backgrounds, it is likely that once enrolled in the service, most of them made the military their career. The rosy picture of the Heraclian emperors deliberately promoting the growth of a small farmer class through the establishment of military freeholders, it is feared, must be consigned largely to the realm of wishful historical thinking.[10]

Nevertheless, it also seems clear that the class of free, small landholders was growing during the Heraclian epoch. Vast changes were taking place in the world of this time; in some areas, although certainly not everywhere, the old Roman system of a peasantry bound to the soil of their masters' estates was disappearing. The rise in population brought about by the influx of Slavs into the Empire may well have been the major factor in this change.[11] In any case, for several centuries of Byzantine history, the nobles would wage a struggle, sometimes secretly, sometimes openly, against the arrangement that permitted the small, free farmers to retain possession of their holdings in the face of the nobles' own landhungry ambitions. The emperors, in most cases, are found upholding the rights of the free peasants and thus attempting to avert the decentralization of authority that results when an aristocracy becomes too powerful.

There are a number of important clues that this view was held by Justinian II. While admittedly the evidence is both complicated and tenuous, the hypothesis that Justinian championed the rights of the small landowners against those of the great aristocrats could be an important key to understanding

[10] The important article by Charanis, "Remarks on Changes in Byzantium," pp. 71–76, is an excellent survey of much recent scholarly work challenging Ostrogorsky's views in this area. Charanis himself basically agrees with Ostrogorsky. See also the important challenge to the "soldier-farmer" interpretation in Kaegi, "Reconsiderations," pp. 40–43.

[11] The role of the Slavs in the agricultural changes in the early medieval Byzantine Empire remains one of the most hotly debated issues in modern Byzantine scholarship. For details, see Paul Lemerle, "Esquisse pour une histoire agraire de Byzance," Revue historique 219 (1958): 63–65, and the same author's earlier study, "Invasions et migrations dans les Balkans depuis la fin de l'époque romaine jusqu'au VIIIe siècle," Revue historique 211 (1954): 265–308.

why he lost his throne. Crucial to the whole question is a document known as the *Nomos Georgikos,* the Farmer's Law, a collection of legal stipulations designed to deal with everyday problems among the free farmer class: boundary disputes, property exchanges, leases, trespassing, hired labor, losses of livestock, theft, and related matters.[12] Many modern scholars have identified the compilation as a work of Justinian II, and if so it is a very important piece of evidence for his intelligent and concerned statesmanship.[13] On the other hand, there are some authorities who deny that Justinian had anything at all to do with the Farmer's Law.[14]

The matter is worth examining in some detail. At the outset, it should be noted that there is almost no dispute about the date of the Farmer's Law; it is universally agreed to come from the late seventh or early eighth century. Thus even if it is not Justinian II's work, it reflects the world of his time. Of utmost significance is the fact that the rural classes described in the document are not serfs bound to the estates of great landowners, but on the contrary are property owners in their own right. While each rural village or commune is regarded as a unit for tax purposes, the individual peasant families retain ownership of their own small plots of land—the very

[12] The Greek text, with critical annotations and English translation and commentary, can be found in Walter Ashburner, "The Farmer's Law," *Journal of Hellenic Studies* 30 (1910): 85–108, and 32 (1912): 68–95.

[13] This hypothesis was brought to the attention of modern Byzantinists by Georges Vernadskij, "Sur les origines de la Loi agraire byzantine," *Byzantion* 2 (1925): 172–73. The ascription has been enthusiastically accepted by Ostrogorsky, *History of the Byzantine State,* pp. 90–91. In a recent work, *Byzantium: The Imperial Centuries,* p. 53, Jenkins states that the Farmer's Law is "almost universally attributed" to Justinian II.

[14] Especially Franz Dölger, "Ist der Nomos Georgikos ein Gesetz des Kaisers Justinian II?" *Festschrift für Leopold Wenger,* 2 vols. (Munich, 1944–45), 2:21–48, and more recently Lemerle, "Esquisse," pp. 49–55, and Johannes Karayannopulos, "Entstehung und Bedeutung des Nomos Georgikos," *Byzantinische Zeitschrift* 51 (1958): 357–73. Ostrogorsky, *History of the Byzantine State,* pp. 90–91, gives a significant survey of the arguments of these and other scholars but states himself unconvinced by them.

situation that tended to infuriate the land-hungry aristocratic owners of large estates.

One of the major arguments for assigning the *Nomos Georgikos* to Justinian II comes from the inscription which forms the heading of the work: "Chapters of the Farmer's Law according to an extract from the Book of Justinian." When the *Nomos* first began to attract scholarly attention in modern times, it was assumed that this was a reference to the great lawgiver, Justinian I, but there are several very strong arguments against such an identification. First, a number of items in the *Nomos Georgikos* actually contradict Justinian I's code, and the *Nomos* as a whole plainly reflects agrarian conditions of a period somewhat later than his reign.[15] The free, mobile peasantry presupposed by the law belongs to an era not any earlier than the Heraclian epoch. Moreover, when citations from the legislation of Justinian I were made in later Byzantine legal works, the standard form for introducing such a citation required listing of the Institutes, Digests, Codex, and Novella "of the great Justinian." The phrase at the heading of the *Nomos Georgikos*, however, speaks only of one "book" of Justinian and omits the epithet "great."[16] In view of these arguments, the theory that the *Nomos Georgikos* is a work of Justinian II has much to commend it. Nor is there anything out of the ordinary in the fact that the emperor's name has no imperial number attached to it in the heading of the document. The official use of imperial numbers was extremely rare at this early period; there is in fact no indication that Justinian ever used the designation "the Second" officially. It never seems to have occurred to him that anyone could possibly confuse him with Justinian I.

Thus if the reference to "Justinian" in the heading of the *Nomos* is to be taken literally at all, it is probably a reference to Justinian II, and scholarly efforts to assign it to any other

[15] Vernadskij, "La Loi agraire," p. 172; Kenneth M. Setton, "On the Importance of Land Tenure and Agrarian Taxation in the Byzantine Empire," *American Journal of Philology* 74 (1953): 233–34.

[16] Ostrogorsky, *History of the Byzantine State*, pp. 90–91.

emperor have been largely abandoned.[17] Those who believe that Justinian had nothing to do with the *Nomos* argue rather that it was a private compilation, not an imperial one, and that the name Justinian appeared in the heading merely because tradition ascribed so much legislation to Justinian I.[18] If this argument is accepted, the *Nomos* merely reflects already established customs and practices of the time rather than imperial efforts to protect the rights of the small landholders.

It is unfortunate that the question is not solved conclusively, nor does it seem likely to be unless some new bits of evidence should come to light. Still, the possibility that the *Nomos* could be Justinian II's work is a matter worth keeping in mind as wider consideration is taken of the mounting tensions within his capital that were to lead to his overthrow.

[17] The noted nineteenth-century Byzantine legal historian K. E. Zachariä von Lingenthal sought to attribute the Farmer's Law to Leo III and Constantine V. This hypothesis was soundly refuted by Ashburner, "Farmer's Law," *J.H.S.* 32:68–71.

[18] Dölger, "Nomos Georgikos," p. 48; Lemerle, "Esquisse," p. 54.

12

FINANCE MINISTERS AND
ARISTOCRATS

Accord according to the chronicler's reports, by far the most serious offenses of Justinian in his first reign resulted from the harsh policies of his finance ministers.[1] Apparently because his own major interests lay in the areas of military and religious policy, the basileus entrusted the details of financial administration to subordinates. Some scholars have seen in the extensive powers he allowed to these officials a deliberate parallel to the activities of Justinian I and his notorious prefect, John of Cappadocia.[2] Whether Justinian II was conscious of this similarity is uncertain, but in any case, his finance ministers eventually incurred great public odium. Particularly unsavory were Stephen, a Persian eunuch, who was *sacellarius* (keeper of the privy purse), and Theodotos, an ex-monk, the general logothete (imperial treasurer). Concerning Stephen, Nikephoros and Theophanes report one of those incidental bits of scandal that are the delight of many chroniclers: reputedly, the *sacellarius* once whipped Justinian's mother, Anastasia, with leather thongs "as a schoolmaster might whip a pupil."[3] What Anastasia had done to pro-

[1] Nikephoros, p. 37; Theophanes, p. 367.
[2] J. B. Bury, *A History of the Later Roman Empire from Arcadius to Irene*, 2 vols. (London, 1889), 2:330.
[3] Nikephoros, p. 37; Theophanes, p. 367.

voke this outburst is not recorded; and although Theophanes does add that the emperor himself was away when the incident took place, Stephen apparently suffered no loss of imperial favor afterward. It is possible that Theophanes' narrative has enlarged upon the original account, for Nikephoros in his version of what happened adds the ambiguous phrase "*en schēmati*," which could mean that Stephen's whipping of the empress was "in semblance" only.[4]

But whatever punishment may have been inflicted on Anastasia, there is little question that Theodotos and Stephen were expert at devising harsh means for extorting funds from the Byzantine aristocracy. Although the chroniclers do not specifically say so, it seems clear that these efforts were part of a planned attempt to crush the excessive power of the great landowning families. It has already been suggested that the emperor's large-scale scattering of military colonists in Asia Minor was one measure by which he hoped to curtail the growth of great landed estates and the feudalizing tendencies that accompanied it; it seems that the policies of his finance ministers were another. In practically every account where Justinian's unpopular measures are mentioned, it is expressly stated that it was the "nobles," the "patricians," who were the chief victims,[5] and in the end it was a representative of this class, the patrician Leontios, who brought about Justinian's downfall.

But even if Justinian II's measures were aimed at the very sensible object of preventing the rise of overmighty subjects and the woes that accompany such a situation, the methods reputedly used by his ministers are deplorable. Theodotos is said to have suspended some of his victims over fires for

---

[4] Thomas Hodgkin, *Italy and Her Invaders*, 8 vols. (Oxford, 1895), 6:359, sets forth this possibility. Hodgkin himself, however, opts for Theophanes' account as a clarification of Nikephoros's and proof that Anastasia received a "genuine whipping."

[5] So noted M. V. Levčenko, "Venety i prasiny v Vizantii v V-VII vv." ["Blues and Greens in Byzantium in the Fifth to Seventh Centuries"], *Vizantiiskii Vremenik* 1 (1947): 182–83. See also Ostrogorsky, *History of the Byzantine State*, pp. 139–40.

slow torture. A number of persons, moreover, were imprisoned for long terms, a practice which had not often been employed by the Byzantine emperors before this time.[6] When Justinian was deposed in 695, the imperial prison was full of these political offenders, some of whom had been there for seven or eight years.

On the other hand, while Justinian's finance ministers seem to have been guilty of gross cruelties, it is highly possible that one very constructive financial policy, a widespread tax reform, is also attributable to Justinian's reign.[7] Evidence is unfortunately very meager on this reform, although it had important repercussions in its impact on the breakdown in the old forms of serfdom that had existed since late Roman times. In the Roman Empire since the reign of Diocletian, the *capitatio* (head tax) and *iugatio* (land tax) were administered together, a system which conduced to bondage to the soil. The last definite instance of such a tax being a functional part of imperial financial administration dates from early in Justinian II's first reign (687), when he remitted Pope Conon's obligation for its payment.[8] Some time between 687 and the reign of the Emperor Nikephoros I (802–811) the system was completely revised; the head tax was replaced by a hearth tax (*to kapnikon*) levied on family units, and this was distinctly separated from the tax on land (*hē synonē*). It would of course be misleading to state that the reform caused the breakdown of serfdom, for in some areas bondage to the soil was already breaking down to such extent that the old system had become impractical. That the reform helped to promote peas-

[6] See E. W. Brooks, "The Successors of Heraclius," *Cambridge Medieval History,* vol. 2 (Cambridge, 1936), p. 409.

[7] Important monographs on this subject are Ernst Stein, "Vom Altertum im Mittelalter zur Geschichte der byzantinischen Finanzverwaltung," *Vierteljahrschrift für Sozial- und Wirtschaftsgeschichte* 21 (1928): 158–70; George Ostrogorsky, "Das Steuersystem im byzantinischen Altertum und Mittelalter," *Byzantion* 6 (1931): 229–40; Setton, "Land Tenure and Agrarian Taxation," pp. 225–59. See also Ostrogorsky, *History of the Byzantine State,* p. 137.

[8] *Liber Pontificalis,* 1:369. See above, chapter 8.

ant mobility, however, seems unquestionable, and in this result it may well have enraged many of the great aristocrats who hoped to keep the tenants residing on their lands in a state of bondage to the soil.

For the purposes of our investigation, a more immediate question is whether or not the tax reform was the work of the Emperor Justinian II. If the *Nomos Georgikos* dates from this time, as is likely, it would provide the key to the problem. In the *Nomos*, although there is some ambiguity in the terms used, it appears that the old system is no longer in use; the hearth tax and the land tax are distinctly separate items.[9] Further scholarly study has deduced some additional clues for assigning the tax reform to Justinian II. The new system, it is pointed out, almost certainly dates considerably before Nikephoros I, for the references to it in his time indicate that by then it was already a long-established practice. Moreover, there is at least a hint that the reform was already in operation under Leo III (717–741), which if correct, pushes the latest possible date for its inauguration much closer to Justinian II's reign.[10]

Although the scarcity of the evidence on the tax reform means that the assignment of it to Justinian II must remain a hypothesis, it is a credible and attractive one. If it is correct, moreover, it provides a further interesting glimpse into what must have been an aspect of the tension between the basileus and the aristocracy.

[9] Ostrogorsky, "Das Steuersystem," pp. 239–40.
[10] Ibid., pp. 237–39.

13

THE REVOLT OF LEONTIOS

SOME time in 692, the year
of the Arab-Byzantine war, the reliable old soldier Leontios, strategos of the Anatolikon theme, was thrown into prison
by imperial order. No reason is given in the sources to explain
his arrest, but in view of the date and of his previous service
in Armenia, it is very possible that he was the commanding
general at the disastrous battle of Sebastopolis.[1] For the next
three years, Leontios languished in the *praetorium*, the imperial prison. Then in the autumn of 695, Justinian suddenly
ordered his release, appointed him strategos of the newly
founded theme of Hellas in central Greece,[2] furnished him
with troops and with three ships, and commanded him to leave
Constantinople immediately.

According to the chronicles of Nikephoros and Theophanes,[3] Leontios was very depressed over his new assignment. Apparently he believed he was being sent to his death
in a dangerous frontier outpost. Nevertheless, orders were
orders, and Leontios was preparing to depart when two of his
old friends arrived at his quarters for a visit. The two were

[1] So Bury suggests in *Later Roman Empire*, 2:328; also Breckenridge, *Numismatic Iconography*, p. 12.

[2] On the location of the theme of Hellas, see Ostrogorsky, *History of
the Byzantine State*, p. 132n8.

[3] The chroniclers' accounts of Leontios's coup are to be found in
Nikephoros, p. 38; Theophanes, pp. 368–69.

monks, Paul and Gregory by name. Paul, like many of his contemporaries, indulged, in spite of the censures of the church,
in the arts of astrology. According to the choniclers, at some
earlier date he had predicted, and Gregory apparently had
enthusiastically seconded the prophecy, that Leontios would
one day become basileus. Predictions of this sort are an excep-
tionally popular theme in Byzantine historical writing and
probably were so in real life as well. In a state where royal
birth was not a prerequisite for wearing the crown, it is little
wonder that dreams of empire enticed many ambitious souls.

In any event, Paul's and Gregory's renewal of their
acquaintance with the despondent strategos provided the
spark that was needed for a sudden *coup d'état*. The methods
reportedly used by Leontios and his associates are astonish-
ingly simple. Late in the evening, with the two monks and the
band of troops entrusted to his command, he went to the *praetorium* where one of his party informed the prefect that "the
basileus" was outside demanding immediate entry. The gates
were opened; Leontios and his followers stormed into the
praetorium, seized and bound the prefect, and proceeded to
free the men who had been Leontios's fellow prisoners. These
naturally were willing recruits for the struggle against Justinian. Meanwhile, according to an additional detail supplied
only by Theophanes, word was being circulated in the city
that Justinian was planning a general massacre of the entire
population and that the Patriarch Kallinikos was destined to be
the first victim. This rumor seems utterly groundless, although
it is impossible to determine whether it is fictional dressing
from one of Theophanes' "lost sources" or whether such a
warning was actually circulated on the night of Leontios's
coup.

Kallinikos, in any case, was convinced to throw in his lot
with the rebels. A cry was raised throughout the city urging
the people to convene at Hagia Sophia, and soon thousands
swarmed into the great church. There the Patriarch Kallinikos
proclaimed Leontios emperor and pronounced: "This is the
day which the Lord hath made!" while the crowds chanted

wildly, "Let Justinian's bones be dug up!" This cry, of course, was not meant to be taken literally, since Leontios's rival was still very much alive. "Dig up his bones!" was simply a Byzantine idiom of deep contempt.[4] The mob was clearly thirsting for blood.

Thus far, the chroniclers' narratives of Leontios's *coup* are disarmingly straightforward. Details of the intrigue which undoubtedly would have made interesting reading are left untold by both Nikephoros and Theophanes, and it is only from a tiny clue in one manuscript version of the mid-ninth-century chronicle of George the Monk that we are able to probe deeper into the nature of Leontios's support. The additional insights that appear at this point are very interesting indeed, for they provide the surprising realization that Leontios's accession was less the spontaneous will of the whole populace than the principal sources would imply. According to George the Monk, "Leontios the Patrician . . . was at night publicly proclaimed Basileus by the *deme* of the Blues."[5]

Historians know a great deal about the activities of the Blues and the Greens, the famous and sometimes notorious Byzantine *demes* or political factions, though the vast bulk of information about them comes from the time before the Heraclians ruled.[6] The two factions were not only bitter rivals in their role as opposing cheering sections in the Hippodrome, they also, and more significantly, represented varying political views, and served as two units which together comprised a citizen militia. Backed up by armed strength, the leaders of the *demes*, cooperatively or separately, often presented demands

[4] Bury, *Later Roman Empire*, 2:329.

[5] The sentence in question was first noted by Levčenko, "Venety i prasiny v Vizantii," p. 182. For further detail see André Maricq, "La Durée du régime des partis populaires à Constantinople," *Bulletin de la Classe des Lettres et Sciences Morales et Politiques*, 5th series, 35 (Brussels, 1949): 66–67.

[6] For a good summary of significant modern scholarship on the nature of the demes see Ostrogorsky, *History of the Byzantine State*, pp. 66–67, 140.

to the emperor in the Hippodrome and received immediate action. Moreover, it was the usual practice for the emperor to align himself openly with one or the other faction.

When the question arises, however, of what the respective factions stood for, modern scholars have tended to walk cautiously. It is certainly an oversimplification to see the Blues as the aristocratic faction and the Greens as the common people, for aristocrats and commoners alike were found in both parties. A more penetrating examination of the differences between the *demes* sees the Blues as led by members of the old, landowning aristocracy, the senatorial families who traced their ancestry back to Graeco-Roman times, while the Green leadership was drawn from the court functionaries—treasury officials and other civil servants—and from the prosperous businessmen of the Empire.[7] Little wonder, then, that Leontios found warm support from the Blues! And yet, if his proclamation as emperor was largely the work of one faction, we have also to surmise that the Greens were still partisans of Justinian —unsuccessful partisans, as it would turn out, but on his side nonetheless.

There is no direct information in any of the sources as to how Justinian was captured, but probably the armed followers of Leontios who gathered outside the palace so far outnumbered Justinian's bodyguard that the young emperor was simply trapped.

Early in the morning following the night of the *coup*, the mob of Leontios's supporters gathered in the Hippodrome and Justinian was brought before them, along with Theodotos and Stephen, the cruel and much-despised finance ministers. The fallen emperor's two henchmen were bound by the feet and soon would be dragged through the streets and then burned to death. For Justinian, however, his successor decided on a more "merciful" sentence, recalling, we are told, his long friendship with Justinian's father, Constantine IV. Let Justinian's life be spared, he decreed, but let him be so disfigured that he might never again aspire to imperial grandeur.

[7] Ibid., p. 67.

Leontios had spoken, and without further ado, Justinian II was subjected to the frightening acts of *rhinokopia* and *glossotomia*, mutilation of the nose and tongue, before the bloodthirsty mobs in the Hippodrome.[8]

He was twenty-six years old, and his world had fallen apart.

We have no completely reliable knowledge of the immediate aftermath. Perhaps Leontios believed Justinian would die, for *rhinokopia* at times proved fatal. According to one account supplied by the rather imaginative Western chronicler Agnellus of Ravenna, the mutilated Justinian, unconscious from loss of blood, was cast out on a lonely beach.[9] Agnellus's report is probably of little historical value here, however, for we know that Leontios soon added to Justinian's penalty a sentence of lifelong exile in Cherson, a desolate port city in the Crimea, the veritable end of the earth.

So Justinian was shipped off to begin his exile, while the Emperor Leontios reigned securely and as the chroniclers say, "there was peace on all sides," for the time being.

Little is known of the reign of Leontios. His round, complacent face with short, bristling beard is among the most lifelike of Byzantine coin effigies (Figure 7), but what he was like as a man or as emperor is difficult to determine. One intriguing detail that has come to light through modern research has to do with his futile attempts to change his name from Leontios to Leo.[10] This whim was no doubt prompted by the fact that Leo was the name of two previous emperors, while the only other Leontios who had ever come near the imperial throne was a pretender who had risen against the Emperor

---

[8] Nikephoros, p. 39; Theophanes, p. 369. For further detail on judicial mutilation see also R. S. Lopez, "Byzantine Law in the Seventh Century," *Byzantion* 16 (1942–43): 454–56.

[9] Agnellus of Ravenna, "De Sancto Felice," *Liber Pontificalis Ecclesiae Ravennatis*, ed. O. Holder-Egger, Monumenta Germaniae Historica: Scriptores Rerum Langobardicarum et Italicarum Saec. VI–IX (Hanover, 1878), p. 366.

[10] J. P. C. Kent, "The Mystery of Leontius II," *Numismatic Chronicle*, 6th series, 14 (1954): 217–18.

FIGURE 7
Leontios; coin of his reign, 695–698
Dumbarton Oaks Collection

Zeno and been crushed two centuries earlier. Leontios had his new name Leo imprinted on his coins and apparently used it in all his official documents. Still, the Byzantine chroniclers of later years stubbornly continued to call him Leontios, and so he is destined to remain, for to call him by the name he preferred would necessitate giving him the imperial number III and the subsequent renumbering of all the successive Leo's on the Byzantine throne.

Leontios's failure even to secure permanent recognition of his new name is indicative of his small impact on history.[11]

---

[11] It should be noted, however, that the Western sources such as the *Liber Pontificalis*, Bede, and Paul the Deacon invariably refer to him as "Leo."

His reign was destined to be short, and like that of his immediate predecessor, to end in disaster.

Before these events took place, however, Justinian II arrived in Cherson to begin serving his life sentence.

14

CHERSON AND KHAZARIA

THE ancient city of Cherson of the Crimea might well be called the Byzantine Empire's last frontier; founded by Greek traders centuries earlier, it remained a stronghold of Hellenism in the midst of primitive and barbarian neighbors.[1] Because of its great distance from the capital at Constantinople, the Byzantine emperors allowed Cherson considerable local autonomy. Its government, in fact, was something of an anachronism; the Chersonites managed their affairs with the fierce spirit of local independence that had characterized the city states of ancient Greece. Because of its remote location, Cherson had also proved useful to the Byzantine emperors as a place of banishment for political prisoners. The Byzantines tended to envision the city on the storm-tossed coast of the Black Sea as a place of utter desolation and misery. That these impressions were not unfounded finds vivid confirmation in the letters of Pope Martin I, exiled there by Justinian's grandfather, Constans, in the mid-seventh century. In Cherson, commented Pope Martin, bread was talked about, but had never been seen.[2]

[1] For background on Cherson see Ellis H. Minns, *Scythians and Greeks* (Cambridge, 1913), pp. 505–43 *passim*, which contains a detailed summary of Russian archaeological work there in the nineteenth and early twentieth century.

[2] Alexander A. Vasiliev, *History of the Byzantine Empire* (Madison, Wis., 1952), p. 224.

Such was the place where the ex-emperor Justinian was banished, and where ultimately he would arouse great alarm among the city fathers.

None of our sources has much to tell us of Justinian at this point. There is no clear description, for instance, of the extent of the injuries inflicted upon him. It is clear, at least, that *glossotomia* had done him little if any harm; his ability to speak was not impaired. (In fact, he appears to have been unusually takative.) His nose, however, was another matter; though the wounds healed, the damage was so pronounced that forever afterwards he would be known as *Rhinokopimenos* or *Rhinotmetos,* the man with the cut-off nose. Agnellus of Ravenna reports that Justinian wore an artificial nose of "pure gold" to cover his disfigurement,[3] but we are given no clue as to how he held on this prosthetic device or where he obtained it. As an exile, it seems rather unlikely that he had access to much pure gold, and perhaps this adornment came only later when his fortunes improved.

The conditions of Justinian's daily life in Cherson are likewise left extremely vague in the chronicle sources. He was not a prisoner in the strict sense of the word, for he had freedom to roam about the town and apparently to talk to whomever he pleased. In time, the deposed sovereign developed something of a following among some of the Chersonites, adventurous young men who must have listened spellbound to his wild schemes of reclaiming his throne and who ultimately would risk their lives for him.

Probably Justinian lived in a monastery, for the cloister frequently provided refuge for political outcasts. But certainly he did not become a monk, for had he done so, his enemies would not have let slip the chance later on to denounce him for broken vows. We do know that among his devoted followers was a certain Abbot Cyrus, who the sources say "cared for" him in the years of his exile and predicted his

[3] Agnellus, p. 367.

recovery of his lost empire.[4] Probably Cyrus's encouragement played a significant role in keeping alive in Justinian a strong determination not to accept his deposition as final.

Meanwhile in Constantinople, the Emperor Leontios had not long to retain his hold on the crown he had seized.[5] In 698, the great North African city of Carthage fell to the Moslems. When efforts to restore Byzantine rule there turned out unsuccessfully, the leaders of the defeated Byzantine fleet determined to rebel against Leontios and set up a new emperor rather than return to their master with news of their failure. The choice for this dangerous appointment was a *drungarius* (naval officer)[6] with the Germanic name of Apsimar, a name altogether unsuited to the imperial dignity. Obligingly, he agreed to change it to Tiberius.[7]

When the rebel fleet appeared in the waters off Constantinople, the Green faction inside the capital city joined the uprising against Leontios, and ultimately Constantinople fell

[4] It is from Justinian's contemporary, the English scholar Bede the Venerable, that we hear that Cyrus was an abbot in "Pontus" who "cared for Justinian in exile." Bede, *De Sex Huius Saeculi Aetatibus*, ed. Theodore Mommsen, Monumenta Germaniae Historica: Auct. Antiq., vol. 13 (Berlin, 1898), p. 317. Nikephoros, p. 42, and Theophanes, p. 375, both report that Cyrus predicted Justinian's restoration, but they confuse the matter by stating that he was from Amastris, a town due south of Cherson on the opposite shore of the Black Sea. Since we have no hint that Justinian ever went to Amastris, it seems probable that Cyrus left there and went to Cherson. Cyrus incidentally would later become Patriarch of Constantinople.

[5] For details of Leontios's fall and Tiberius Apsimar's reign see Nikephoros, pp. 39–40, and Theophanes, pp. 369–72.

[6] Apsimar was *drungarius* of the Cibyrrheotes, the title *drungarius* being roughly equivalent to that of commodore. Antoniadis-Bibicou, *Études d'histoire maritime*, p. 84.

[7] He is counted either as Tiberius II or III by modern historians, the difference caused by uncertainty whether the first-century Roman emperor Tiberius (A.D. 14–37) should be assigned the imperial number I. In view of this confusion it seems better to follow the practice of the early sources, who frequently call Leontios's successor by both his regnal name and his original one, Tiberius Apsimar.

into the rebels' hands.[8] Tiberius Apsimar was properly conse-
crated basileus by the same obliging Patriarch Kallinikos who
had performed Leontios's coronation three years earlier. The
fallen Leontios was subjected to rhinokopia and forced to enter
a local monastery.

No doubt encouraged by these events, the impetuous Justinian began to speak more and more openly about his plans
to regain the throne, and eventually the local governmental
authorities in Cherson began to feel that his outspoken boast-
ing was a menace to the city's well-being. The Chersonite city
fathers thus decided that Justinian was so dangerous he should
either be killed or shipped back to Tiberius Apsimar and strict
imprisonment in the capital.[9] Although nothing is known of
the particular circumstances, we do know that Justinian was
warned in time of these plans, and fled northward to Doros, a
town held by the Goths of the Crimea,[10] and not far from the
lands of the Khazars. From Doros, Justinian sent word to
Ibouzeros Gliabanos,[11] the Khagan of the Khazars, appealing
for refuge and presenting his hopes of eventually regaining
his empire. The year of Justinian's flight from Cherson was
probably 704; he was now in his mid-thirties and had spent
almost a decade in Cherson. But the confidence that he was
the only rightful emperor of Byzantium was as strong in him

[8] The involvement of the Greens in Tiberius Apsimar's successful
coup is known only from a thirteenth-century Byzantine manuscript
known as *Anonyme de Cumont*, probably a copy of a much earlier (ninth-
century?) work. For further detail see Maricq, "La Durée du régime des
partis populaires," pp. 67–68.

[9] Nikephoros, p. 40; Theophanes, p. 372.

[10] Also called Daras. Alexander A. Vasiliev, *The Goths in the Crimea*
(Cambridge, Mass., 1936), p. 81.

[11] This is the Greek version of the khagan's name as preserved in
some manuscripts of the *Parastaseis Syntomoi Chronikai*, an anonymous
writing of the mid-eighth century in J.-P. Migne, ed., Patrologiae Cursus
Completus: Series Graeca, vol. 157 (Paris, 1866), col. 678. The Khazar
form underlying the Greek spelling is not definitely known. D. M. Dunlop,
A History of the Jewish Khazars (Princeton, 1954), p. 171, suggests Busir
for the first part. M. I. Artamonov, *Historia Khazar* (Leningrad, 1962),
p. 196, calls him Ibuzir-Glavan.

FIGURE 8
Tiberius Apsimar; coin of his reign, 698–705
Dumbarton Oaks Collection

as ever; the passing years had indeed probably deepened his resolve to regain the throne he had lost or die in the attempt.

The Khazars, to whom Justinian appealed for aid, are a mysterious people; modern scholars as well as medieval sources find many points of disagreement about them.[12] According to some authorities, they were an oriental race, with the slanting eyes, black hair, and dark skin typical of many of the peoples of central Asia. One medieval Arab writer, however, pictured them in very different terms: "Their complexions are white, their eyes blue, their hair flowing and predomi-

[12] Dunlop, *Khazars*, is the most detailed study in English. More recent is the Russian work by Artamonov, *Historia Khazar*.

nantly reddish, their bodies large and their nature cold. Their general aspect is wild."[13] On the last point, at least, authorities would generally agree. More than two hundred years after Justinian's time, when the Khazar empire had grown to a position of great eminence in world affairs, the Byzantine emperor Constantine VII still regarded them as utter barbarians. *Never marry a Khazar,* warned Constantine VII in a book of advice to his son and heir;[14] the disparity of such a "mixed marriage" was simply too disgraceful in Byzantine eyes.

Some of the Khazars, it seems, were nomads who dwelt in tents of felt, but as their power and prestige grew, many of them settled in clay houses and the ruling family is said to have resided in a brick palace. The principal foods of Khazars of all classes were rice and fish. Their native language was a dialect somewhat similar to Turkish.[15] Religiously they were pagans, though a number of years after Justinian's sojourn among them, the leadership of the tribe converted en masse to Judaism. This strange twist of fate fascinated medieval Jews in other lands, who tended to believe their Khazar brethren represented one of the lost tribes of Israel.

The Byzantine accounts of Justinian's visit to Khazaria provide some of the clearest glimpses of the Khazar state at this point in its history. Already they controlled a vast area, including a number of fortified cities along the northern coasts of the Black Sea, areas now a part of southern Russia. The khagan of Justinian's time, the ambitious, scheming Ibouzeros Gliabanos, was clearly a useful man to have as an ally.

When Ibouzeros agreed to give him refuge, the fugitive Rhinotmetos left Doros for the Khazar court. For the first time in years, he was to find himself treated with imperial honors. A formal alliance was drawn up between the Khazars and the ex-emperor, and as a binding token of friendship, the khagan

[13] Dunlop, *Khazars,* p. 11.

[14] Constantine VII Porphyrogenitus, *De Administrando Imperio,* pp. 69–73.

[15] Dunlop, *Khazars,* pp. 39, 92–93.

gave his sister to Justinian for a wife.[16] One can only imagine the feelings of the young Khazar princess when informed of her brother's plan for her future. Like many nobly born women through history, she had probably realized all her life that she was destined to be a matrimonial pawn in her family's political game. Yet she could have scarcely dreamed that the husband selected for her would be a disfigured fugitive, and if she approached the union with fear and disappointment, one could hardly blame her.

There is no direct information as to what sort of marriage ceremony was performed for Justinian and his Khazar bride, but in view of his staunch orthodoxy, Justinian in all likelihood insisted on Christian rites. In any event, it is clear that sooner or later he decided to have his bride baptized into the Christian faith. We do not know with any certainty the lady's original name (one source suggests that it may have been "Chikhak").[17] But at her baptism, she received the name of Theodora, a name that Justinian undoubtedly selected for her himself and one that suggests a great deal about his thinking at this time.

Everyone who knew anything at all about the first Emperor Justinian knew that his empress was called Theodora and that he had been deeply devoted to her. There is a touch of real beauty in the fact that Justinian II should want his bride to have the name that went so well with his own and that recalled so vividly the earlier imperial couple and their faithful and lifelong love for each other. The choice moreover

[16] Nikephoros, p. 40; Theophanes, p. 373. Later Nikephoros (p. 41) speaks of the lady's return to her "father." This is probably a mistake for "brother" but perhaps could indicate either that the khagan's father was still alive even though his son was ruler or that Justinian's bride was the khagan's half-sister.

[17] Constantine VII Porphyrogenitus, *De Cerimoniis*, 1:32, and a note appended to this passage at 2:126–27, provide the clues for determining the original name of Byzantium's "Khazar empress." Apparently her name was the root from which was derived the word *tzitzakia*, a term used for certain state vestments. The Khazar empress in question could well be Justinian II's Theodora, but she could equally well be Irene of the Khazars, wife of Constantine V (740–775). See also Dunlop, *Khazars*, p. 177.

carried with it something of a political manifesto: a statement of the fugitive emperor's determination that Byzantium should once again witness the reign of a Justinian and Theodora. Though most Byzantines would have viewed marriage to a Khazar as a shameful misalliance, Justinian apparently accepted his Khazar lady with pride and affection. Theodora for her part, whatever may have been her misgivings when she entered into matrimony with Justinian, soon must have learned to love him deeply, for in due time she would venture to save his life at considerable risk to her own.

Following their marriage, Justinian and Theodora moved to the fortified city of Phanagoria, near the eastern shore of the Strait of Kertch, one of the chief centers of Khazar influence.[18] Clearly, Ibouzeros was not yet ready to launch an attempt to help Justinian regain the Byzantine throne, but probably this was his long-range plan. Meanwhile, Justinian and his wife lived at Phanagoria for some time until word of the former emperor's whereabouts reached Tiberius Apsimar in Constantinople. Tiberius received this news with alarm and sent a number of requests to the khagan offering a handsome reward for Justinian dead or alive. The khagan at first seems to have ignored these appeals, but after a time, the thoughts of the reward and the good will of the reigning emperor began to outweigh any obligations Ibouzeros might have felt toward his brother-in-law. Craftily, he planned how he might dispatch Justinian. A troop of the khagan's men was sent to Phanagoria, ostensibly as a bodyguard for the deposed monarch, while two high-ranking henchmen of the khagan were instructed that their real mission was to put Justinian to death as soon as a certain signal was received. One of the khagan's slaves, however, learned of the plan and revealed it to Theodora. At this crucial moment, the Khazar girl chose loyalty to her Byzantine husband over any allegiance to her brother. She

[18] This town was later called by the Russians "Tmutarakan," and in modern times is Taman. The latter name is a variant of Tomen, which in Justinian II's time was the port of Phanagoria. Henri Grégoire, "Le Nom de la ville de Tmutarakan," *La Nouvelle Clio* 4 (1952): 288–92.

warned Justinian of the plot, and he in turn summoned one of the would-be assassins, Papatzys, the governor of Phanagoria, a man with whom he had previously been on good terms. While they were alone together, Justinian strangled the Khazar governor with a cord. For the second of the khagan's agents, Balgitzis, governor of the nearby city of Bosporus, Justinian arranged a similar fate very soon thereafter.[19]

Now he knew he would have to flee for his life, but Theodora, who was anticipating the birth of a child, could not be taken along. Together they decided that her best hope of safety would be in returning to Ibouzeros's court. Then Justinian slipped away to the little nearby port of Tomen, and put out to sea in a tiny fishing boat with a few companions.[20]

He was going to reclaim his empire, he said, but even a man of Justinian's indomitable spirit must have realized the near hopelessness of the situation. Behind him lay the land of the Khazars who had proved such unreliable allies, but behind him too lay the woman who loved him and who carried his child. Before him lay only the stormy waters of the Black Sea. He was a fugitive with a price on his head, and marked by scars that would render disguise almost impossible. Into the dark of the night, Justinian Rhinotmetos was sailing toward the grim unknown.

[19] Nikephoros, p. 41; Theophanes, p. 378. The names of Papatzys and Balgitzis are recorded only by Theophanes. Dunlop, *Khazars*, p. 172, notes that "Balgitzis" may simply be a Khazar title indicating "governor."

[20] Possibly including some Khazars. The Armenian chronicler Ghévond says (p. 17) that Justinian's brother-in-law Trouhegh accompanied him on his departure from Khazaria and was later slain in battle outside the walls of Constantinople. Ghévond is very confused on the events leading to Justinian's recovery of his throne, but this report may suggest that there were Khazars, perhaps even some of Theodora and Ibouzeros's kin, among Justinian's followers. See also Artamonov, *Historia Khazar*, p. 197.

15

JUSTINIAN'S RETURN

THE small boat Justinian had appropriated so hastily in Tomen was far too light to risk venturing far out into the open sea. Keeping reasonably close to shore, the party of escapees sailed along the southern coast of the Crimea until they reached their first destination, the port of Symbolon near Cherson. There Justinian felt confident he could recruit support from among his former acquaintances. The ex-emperor did not dare go ashore himself; he would have been too easily recognized. But one of his men slipped into Cherson where he rounded up a small group of volunteers. The Patriarch Nikephoros records the names of two of them in his chronicle: Barasbakourios (who some years later would die for his loyalty to Justinian) and his brother, Salibas. Theophanes, in addition to these, lists three others: Stephen, Moropaulos ("Foolish Paul"), and Theophilos, and seems to suggest that these five made up the total enlistment.[1]

From Symbolon, the plan was to sail along the coast of the Black Sea to the land of the Bulgars. According to a story preserved only by Theophanes, as the boat made its way over the rough waters, a terrible storm arose, so fierce that it seemed impossible to hope for a safe landing. One of Justinian's servants, Myakes, sure that the storm was a sign of divine wrath, fearfully approached him saying, "Behold, master, we

---

[1] Nikephoros, p. 41; Theophanes, p. 373.

are dying. Make a compact with God concerning your safety, that if God restore your sovereignty, you will take vengeance on none of your enemies." To this, Justinian replied, "If I spare any one of them, may God drown me here!"[2] It is not possible to determine if there is historical fact underlying this anecdote, but if it is authentic it is a vivid glimpse of the character of Justinian Rhinotmetos. Whatever he may have lacked of the spirit of gracious forgiveness, he was certainly not deficient in courage, nor was he the sort to be led into a superstitious bargain with the Deity.

In any event, the little boat somehow survived the hazards of the long journey. Sailing past the mouths of the Dnieper and Dniester rivers, the party finally arrived at the mouth of the Danube. From there, Justinian sent an envoy, Stephen (probably one of the Chersonite volunteers), to approach Tervel, the Khan of the Bulgars, on the matter of an alliance. The Bulgars whom Tervel ruled were settled in the area between the Danube and the Haemus Mountains. Although closely related to other Bulgar peoples settled further to the south in Sklavinia, Tervel's subjects seem to have been a distinctly separate group.[3] They were pagans and had only recently migrated into the area. Apparently their civilization was very primitive, but they were able to furnish a large and effective fighting force.

Among the so-called proto-Bulgarian inscriptions of Madara there is an interesting confirmation of Justinian's visit to Tervel's land.[4] The inscription, in poorly spelled Greek, is so badly broken by the ravages of time as to defy complete decipherment. Enough of it is extant, however, to show that it recorded the making of a treaty between Tervel and "the *Rhinokopimenos*" (Justinian). There is a suggestion, too, that

[2] Theophanes, p. 373.

[3] Genoveva Cankova-Petkova, "Bulgarians and Byzantium during the First Decades after the Foundation of the Bulgarian State," *Byzantinoslavica* 24 (1963): 47.

[4] Veselin Beševliev, *Die protobulgarischen Inschriften* (Berlin, 1963), pp. 97–107. See also Cankova-Petkova, "Bulgarians and Byzantium," pp. 43–44.

Justinian tried to get Tervel to enlist the support of other groups of Bulgars in the Sklavinian area, but as the inscription enigmatically comments, apparently in the words of Tervel, "My kinsmen [literally "uncles"] in Thessaloniki did not trust the Emperor with the cut-off nose."[5]

In spite of this apparent failure to win the cooperation of the khan's relations in Sklavinia, Tervel himself willingly received Justinian and his party. The winter of the year 704 was approaching at this juncture and it was decided that any military action should be postponed until the return of warm weather. In the meantime Justinian and Tervel worked out the details of their alliance, including among other promises of future reward the offer of Justinian's daughter to Tervel as a wife.[6] This daughter must have been the child of Justinian and his first wife, Eudokia,[7] although her whereabouts during the ten years of her father's exile are a complete mystery. Justinian probably did not even know if the girl was still alive; and if so, she might well by this time have been married to someone else or irrevocably committed to religious vows. In any case, for causes unknown, this part of the bargain was never to be fulfilled.

With the coming of warm weather in the year 705, Justinian and his Bulgar allies set out toward Constantinople.[8] There for three days they encamped outside the walls, while the astonished Byzantines on the fortifications above them shouted down insulting remarks to the Rhinotmetos. The incredible had happened; the deposed monarch of ten years before was outside the gates with a large army. Still the walls of Constantinople had withstood many an enemy in the past.

---

[5] Beševliev, *Die protobulgarischen Inschriften*, p. 97.

[6] Nikephoros, p. 42; Theophanes, p. 374.

[7] That the daughter promised to Tervel was not Theodora's child was surmised long before knowledge of Justinian's previous marriage came to light. See Hodgkin, *Italy and Her Invaders*, 6:367.

[8] For a detailed challenge to the older view that Justinian's return occurred in summer or autumn of 705 see Constance Head, "On the Date of Justinian II's Restoration," *Byzantion* 39(1969): 104-7.

And Tiberius Apsimar, in the seven years of his reign, had proved himself a capable and courageous leader. . . .

Then on the third night after their arrival, someone uncovered a secret passage under the city's walls. Very likely it was Justinian himself who made this happy discovery, for as a former ruler he would have been in a position to know the secrets of the capital's defenses. The passageway was an old aqueduct or tunnel, and through this dank, underground channel, Justinian led a few of his trusted comrades into the northwest end of the city. The suddenness of their entry enabled them to seize control of the Blachernae area with little effort. The capitulation of the entire city followed not long thereafter, for when he learned of his adversary's entry, Tiberius Apsimar fled in dismay. Justinian posted a reward for Apsimar's capture. The wheel of fate had turned full circle.

It was said that a disfigured man could not reign as emperor, but Justinian Rhinotmetos reigned and none dared say him nay. Established in the palace that had been the home of his youth, clothed again in the magnificent imperial robes of red and purple, and perhaps with his golden nose to hide the scars that time would never erase, Justinian II could pride himself on the fact that he had done what no emperor before him had ever done. Plans for vast changes stirred in his restless brain—vengeance upon his enemies and due rewards for the faithful. And for his greatest love, the greatest reward of all. The restored emperor Justinian II lost no time in dispatching a fleet to the distant shores of the Black Sea to reclaim his empress, Theodora of the Khazars.

16

RESTORATION AND REPRISALS:

THE LION AND THE ASP

WHILE he awaited word from Khazaria, Justinian set about tending to other matters of state. New coins must be released to replace those of Leontios and Apsimar, and for his first issues after his return to the throne, Justinian selected for the obverse a Christ effigy, a practice he had initiated in his first reign and that neither Leontios nor Apsimar had followed. Historians of Byzantine art are intrigued by the fact that the Christ on the coins of Justinian's second reign is a completely different figure from the one he used earlier; a young, curly-haired "Syrian" figure with a very short beard (Figure 9), rather than the Christ with long hair and flowing beard more familiar in the long tradition of Byzantine iconography.[1] Justinian's reason for the change remains unknown, but most likely the "Syrian" Christ-type is a picture of a certain icon that had special significance to him.[2]

On the reverse of the new issues appeared Justinian himself (Figure 10); his portrait is somewhat more stylized than those used in his first reign, but the thin, pointed face is unmis-

---

[1] Breckenridge, *Numismatic Iconography*, passim. See also, Grierson, *Dumbarton Oaks Catalogue*, 2:569, 645; Bellinger, "Gold Coins of Justinian II," pp. 109–10; Kitzinger, "Some Reflections on Portraiture in Byzantine Art," pp. 190–92.

[2] Breckenridge, *Numismatic Iconography*, pp. 97–100.

takably that of the same man. The designers of the new dies showed no flaw in Justinian's nose; the emperor's effigy must be perfect, even if he was not.[3] Dressed in the long, jewelled ceremonial scarf called the *loros*, Justinian appears with a large cross in one hand and an orb inscribed PAX (peace) in the other. Since coins were often used as a medium of conveying imperial propaganda to the people, and since the PAX inscription had very seldom been used on Byzantine coins heretofore, these coins must be seen as the emperor's professed announcement that his restoration would inaugurate a reign of peace within the Empire. The inscription encircling his portrait on these same issues reads D[OMINUS] N[OSTER] IUSTINIANUS MULTUS AN[NOS], "Justinian our lord for many years," and is without precedent among imperial coin legends.[4] In it perhaps is hinted something of the hope and pos-

[3] On this matter see especially André Grabar, *L'Empereur dans l'art byzantin* (Paris, 1936), p. 10. In this connection, it is interesting to notice Richard Delbrück's identification of a certain porphyry head (commonly known as "Carmagnola" and located in St. Mark's in Venice) as a portrait of Justinian II. The statue depicts a crowned, middle-aged man with a rather mutilated nose—mutilation that Delbrück described as a feature of the original sculpture, rather than a result of later damage to it. On this basis, Delbrück built up an intriguing but very tenuous case that the sculpture represents Justinian II; that Justinian underwent some kind of corrective surgery to rebuild his nose, and that although this operation was largely successful, some scars still remained and were depicted with complete realism by the sculptor. For details see Richard Delbrück, "Carmagnola: Porträt eines byzantinischen Kaisers," *Sonderabdruck aus den römischen Mitteilungen des Kaiserlich Deutschen Archäologischen Instituts* 29 (1914): 71–89, and the same author's *Antike Porphyrwerke* (Berlin, 1932), pp. 30, 119. Delbrück's hypothesis, while extremely interesting, lacks any concrete support. Not only is such an operation unattested in any of the written sources, it is highly unlikely, as Grabar has pointed out, that the strongly ingrained traditions of perfection in imperial iconography would have permitted any depiction of Justinian's disfigurement. A further argument against Delbrück's theory is the fact that "Carmagnola" bears no resemblance to Justinian's portrait on his coins: it has a very square face and is clean shaven, while Justinian II's face was thin with a very pointed chin, and as a mature man he is always depicted with a beard.

[4] Breckenridge, *Numismatic Iconography*, pp. 23, 63, 102. As Breckenridge notes, *multus* must be a spelling error for *multos*.

FIGURE 9
Image of Christ ("Syrian" type) used on
coinage of Justinian's second reign
Dumbarton Oaks Collection

sible insecurity that Justinian felt at the time of his restoration.

From the few remaining issues that are dated, we learn something further of Justinian's thinking at this point. As far as he was concerned, the year of his return was the twentieth year of his reign.[5] He had always been emperor; it was as if Leontios and Tiberius Apsimar had never existed.

But they did exist: Leontios, who for seven years now had been a monk, and Apsimar, who unable to escape Justinian's search was found in Apollonias and brought back to Constan-

---

[5] See especially Alfred R. Bellinger, "The Copper of the Second Reign of Justinian II," *American Numismatic Society Museum Notes* 12 (1966): 122; Grierson, *Dumbarton Oaks Catalogue*, 2:644, 654–58.

FIGURE 10
*Justinian II at 36, shortly after his restoration;
coin of his second reign*
Dumbarton Oaks Collection

tinople a prisoner. For them and for a number of those who
had served them too well, Justinian's restoration meant not
peace but the sword.

We now come to the vexed question of the extent of Justinian's reprisals upon his enemies. If we are to take literally
the accounts of Nikephoros, and more especially Theophanes,
Justinian had returned from exile so preoccupied by revenge
as to have neglected the really important aspects of governing
his empire. As will be seen, such an interpretation is scarcely
fair, and there is much in Justinian's second reign to indicate
his constructive statesmanship and genuine concern for his
empire. Nevertheless, the fate he prepared for Leontios and

Apsimar was a spectacular act of vengeance and one that must have made a tremendous impact upon those who witnessed it. On the fifteenth of February, 706,[6] the two ex-emperors were loaded with chains and paraded through the streets of Constantinople and into the Hippodrome. In this great stadium where eleven years earlier he had himself suffered *rhinokopia*, Justinian now sat in imperial splendor. His two rivals were forced to crouch before him while he used them as human footstools, planting one foot upon the neck of each of his fallen foes. During this performance, the audience chanted an appropriate verse from Psalm 91:

> Thou hast trodden on the asp and the basilisk;
> The lion and the dragon thou hast trampled underfoot.[7]

Following this display, which to many Byzantine minds must have seemed a true fulfillment of the scriptural prophecy, the Lion and the Asp, Leontios and Apsimar, were removed and beheaded.

Justinian certainly realized from personal experience that it could be risky to leave a deposed emperor alive. The two former rulers, however, were by no means the only victims of Justinian's purge. Apsimar's brother Heraclius, who had served as a general during Apsimar's reign, was executed, as were a number of other high-ranking officers and nobles. Although the extent of these reprisals is impossible to determine accurately, and, as will be seen, due allowance must be made for exaggeration by the chroniclers, Justinian's purge of the supporters of his fallen rivals still emerges as an ill-considered and violent reaction on his part, and one which robbed the Empire of capable leaders who probably would have served him as loyally as they had served his predecessors.

[6] The date is not recorded by the chroniclers but it is preserved in the Byzantine *Necrologium* cited by Grierson, "The Tombs and Obits of the Byzantine Emperors," p. 52.

[7] Psalm 91, verse 13, quoted by Theophanes, p. 375. This verse is slightly altered in standard English versions of the Bible. On the final humiliation of Leontios and Apsimar, see also Nikephoros, p. 42, an account very similar to Theophanes' but lacking the biblical citation.

Nikephoros and Theophanes are generous with their details on the emperor's methods. Apsimar's brother Heraclius and some of his associates were hanged from the city walls; other victims were marched off to execution after enjoying an imperial banquet; while still others were tied up in sacks weighted with rocks and thrown into the sea.[8] Theophanes' account of these executions, while partially drawn from the same source used by Nikephoros, contains further detail. Theophanes seems especially concerned to emphasize the "unnumbered multitude" of victims and to point out that it included soldiers and citizens as well as nobles, details which are very probably exaggerated. It is notable that both of the Western sources closest to Justinian's lifetime, the *Liber Pontificalis* and Bede's *De Sex Aetatibus*, have practically nothing to say about Justinian's reprisals following his restoration other than recording the execution of "Leo and Tiberius" and the punishment inflicted upon the Patriarch Kallinikos. This is not to deny that other reprisals took place, for certainly they did, yet had they been so extensive as Theophanes indicates, it is odd that they escaped contemporary Western notice so completely. Almost a hundred years later, at the end of the eighth century, when Paul the Deacon was writing his *Historia Langobardorum*, further gruesome detail was being reported in the West about Justinian II; as Paul records, "Leo in banishing him cut off his nostrils and he, after he had assumed the sovereignty, as often as he wiped off his hand flowing with a drop of rheum, almost so often did he order some one of those who had been against him to be slain."[9] Paul's source for this item is unknown; there is apparently no direct parallel in the extant Byzantine sources, yet it is suggestive of a growing anti-Justinian legend, possibly emanating from Byzantium in the decades following Justinian's death.

[8] Nikephoros, pp. 42–43; Theophanes, p. 375.

[9] Paul the Deacon, *Historia Langobardorum*, VI, xxxii, ed. L. Bethmann and G. Waitz, Monumenta Germaniae Historica: Scriptores Rerum Langobardicarum et Italicarum Saec. VI–IX (Hanover, 1878), p. 175; English trans. William Dudley Foulke, *History of the Langobards* (Philadelphia, 1906), p. 275.

Rather than accepting such accounts of wholesale reprisals too literally, it is much more reasonable to believe that
Justinian's purges were largely a continuation of the anti-
aristocratic policies of his first reign. Several non-Greek Eastern sources contain significant emphasis on the anti-aristocratic
orientation of the restored emperor's reprisals.[10] Even here,
the frequent mention of patricians in the emperor's service
later in his reign warns against too literal interpretation of the
chroniclers' reports.

Further significant doubt concerning the great number
of victims arises from the striking fact that Justinian did not
execute one of the most potentially dangerous persons in the
Empire: Theodosius, the son of Tiberius Apsimar. The historical accounts hostile to Justinian do not mention this surprising
act of mercy. We only become aware of it by the fact that some
years later Theodosius, son of Apsimar, rose to great promi-
nence as the iconoclastic bishop of Ephesus and confidant of
the emperors Leo III and Constantine V.[11] Why Justinian chose
to spare him we do not know; yet the fact that Theodosius did
survive is in striking disharmony with the accounts that por-
tray Justinian slaying all his enemies, real and imagined, with
careless abandon.

For the Patriarch Kallinikos, who had performed the coro-
nations of both Leontios and Apsimar, Justinian decreed the
penalty of blinding.[12] This punishment, terrible as it was, was
standard procedure in the early medieval period, both in
Byzantium and the West, and was considered a merciful sub-

[10] Several non-Greek Eastern sources contain significant emphasis on
the anti-aristocratic orientation of the restored Justinian's purge. Michael
the Syrian, 2:478, states that Justinian executed "many of the great ones"
and sent others into exile. Similar comments are found in Gregorius Abû'l
Faraj, 1:105; *Chronicon ad Anno Domini 846 Pertinens*, trans. from Syriac
by E. W. Brooks (Louvain, 1955), p. 175; Mas'ûdi, *Le Livre de l'avertis-
sement*, trans. B. Carra de Vaux (Paris, 1897), p. 225. See also Levčenko,
"Venety i prasiny," p. 182.

[11] Theophanes, p. 427; also letter of Pope Gregory II in Mansi,
Concilia, vol. 12, cols. 967–68.

[12] On the fall of Kallinikos and the appointment of Cyrus see Nikephoros, p. 42; Theophanes, p. 375; Bede, *De Sex Aetatibus*, p. 317.

stitute for the death sentence. Kallinikos was then shipped off
to Rome. Many historians have assumed that he was to serve
as a warning to Pope John VII that he must negotiate with
Justinian concerning the still unsolved problem of the Quinisext Canons, but this is merely a conjecture. As the replace-
ment for Kallinikos, Justinian chose the Abbot Cyrus, the monk
who had encouraged him in the days of his exile and who
had predicted his restoration to the throne. Here, as elsewhere, Justinian's vigorous methods against his enemies were
matched by devoted loyalty to those he counted as his true
friends.

The element of steadfastness in Justinian's character is
seen most clearly in his devotion to his Khazar bride. Justinian's loyalty to Theodora is a fact apparent even in the sources
which generally evaluate him adversely, and has often been
commented upon by modern historians. One can easily imagine
the astonishment and disapproval felt by many Byzantines
when they learned that their emperor was married to a *Khazar*;
the idea of a foreign-born, barbarian empress was as much a
departure from tradition as that of a disfigured emperor.[13]
Because of this Byzantine sense of superiority and in view, too,
of the treacherous conduct of the Khagan Ibouzeros, it would
not have been surprising if Justinian had repudiated his Khazar marriage. Instead, as we have seen, he sent for Theodora
as soon as possible after his restoration. He had no way of
knowing, of course, if she was even alive, if she had survived
the rigors of childbirth. And would Ibouzeros let her go? Probably fearful that her brother would try to hinder Theodora's
departure, Justinian decided upon a show of force and sent a
large fleet to conduct her to Constantinople. The impressive
size of the expedition was no doubt designed, too, as a note of
warning to Ibouzeros that Justinian had not forgotten his
betrayal, and perhaps as a foretaste of policy moves that the
restored emperor was already planning for the future.

[13] Theodora's status as the first foreign-born Byzantine empress is
pointed out by George Ostrogorsky, "The Byzantine Empire in the World
of the Seventh Century," *Dumbarton Oaks Papers* 13 (1959): 18.

According to a story told only by Theophanes, a storm struck the fleet on its way to Khazaria and the losses were tremendous. When the khagan learned of this development, he reputedly sent Justinian an insulting letter, opening with the rebuke: "O fool! Should you not have sent just two or three ships to fetch your wife and not killed such a multitude? Or did you think you would have to take her by force? Behold, a son is born to you," the khagan continued. "Now send and take them both."[14]

Justinian apparently was willing to ignore his brother-in-law's bad temper, and subsequently sent a much smaller party headed by Theophylaktos the *cubicularius* (chamberlain) to the land of the Khazars. At last Theodora arrived safely in Constantinople, bringing with her the little son who was born in Justinian's absence.

The boy's name was Tiberius.

None of the sources gives any explanation why this—of all names—should have been chosen for Justinian's heir; it is in fact one of the most baffling of mysteries connected with his entire history. It seems almost incredible that Justinian would have deliberately selected the name of his hated predecessor for his son, and though Justinian himself had had an uncle Tiberius, that prince's unhappy fate would scarcely have commended itself to such a memorial. More likely the choice was Theodora's. At the time she gave birth to the infant in Khazaria, she probably felt that she would never see his father again; on the other hand, Tiberius Apsimar might well declare the child's life forfeit because of his dangerous proximity to the throne. So why not call him Tiberius and hope that in naming him for the emperor his life would be safer? This explanation, it must be noted, is based on mere conjecture. In any event, Justinian apparently raised no objections to his little son's name, and the fact that he allowed it to go unchanged may be indicative of a more level-headed view of the past than the chroniclers are willing to admit of him.

The coronation of Theodora and Tiberius followed soon

[14] Theophanes, p. 375.

FIGURE 11
Justinian II with his son and co-emperor, Tiberius
(reverse of coin in Figure 9)
Dumbarton Oaks Collection

after their arrival. According to the long-standing custom, Justinian himself placed the crowns upon the heads of his wife and their son. The infant Tiberius was officially proclaimed basileus to reign with his father. Co-emperors were frequent in the Byzantine state, but rarely had there been one so young. Justinian probably felt that this move would help secure his own position. Perhaps he feared, too, that there would be antagonism to the succession of a half-Khazar prince to the Byzantine throne and that the coronation of Tiberius at an early age would insure against later difficulties.

Some measure of Justinian's pride in his son is glimpsed

in the delightful coin designs that were brought into use after Tiberius's coronation. Justinian and his little son are depicted side by side, wearing identical robes and crowns. Between them, they hold a large ceremonial cross (Figure 11).[15]

Of Theodora's transformation from barbarian princess to Byzantine empress the sources tell us practically nothing.[16] One of the few references to her in the extant literature, however, does provide an important clue to the further development of her husband's Khazar policy. According to this report, Justinian set up a large pair of statues of himself and Theodora in a prominent part of the palace. When the Khagan Ibouzeros Gliabanos visited Constantinople not long thereafter, the account continues, it was his custom to sit at the feet of his sister's statue.[17] This clue indicates that whatever Justinian may have thought of his brother-in-law's past treachery, he was for the time being at least ready to receive him as an ally. Another strange contradiction to the general idea that Justinian was determined to take rapid vengeance upon all his foes!

[15] See Grierson, *Dumbarton Oaks Catalogue*, vol. 2, plates 43–44.

[16] For a strange distortion of the story of Justinian and Theodora, perhaps as retold and embellished by the Bulgars, see Marius Canard, "Les Aventures d'un prisonnier arabe et d'un patrice byzantin à l'époque des guerres bulgaro-byzantines," *Dumbarton Oaks Papers* 9–10 (1956): 49–72, esp. pp. 69–70.

[17] *Parastaseis Syntomoi Chronikai*, cols. 678–79. See also Dunlop, *Khazars*, p. 173. An additional intriguing detail recorded in the *Parastaseis* is the fact that between the statues of the imperial couple was an immense statue of an elephant.

17

THE QUEST FOR ALLIES

J USTINIAN'S acceptance of
Ibouzeros Gliabanos as an ally is but one aspect of a larger
theme running throughout his second reign: the building up of
a strong system of foreign alliances. In the long run, Justinian's
quest for allies would prove of little enduring worth, yet the
fact that he made such attempts at all is a sign of concerned
statesmanship.

Among the most pressing matters demanding Justinian's
attention immediately after his restoration was that of suitable
rewards for Tervel the Bulgar. Because of the lucky discovery
of the secret passage and the ensuing panic his appeance had
caused in Constantinople, Justinian apparently had not had to
allow Tervel's Bulgar armies to enter his capital. Still, a bargain was a bargain; and Tervel and his hosts were camped
outside the city walls awaiting their rewards.

There has been much scholarly controversy over Justinian's gifts to the Bulgars. Though some late writers indicate
that the emperor actually ceded the Byzantine province of
Zagorje "beyond the mountains" to the Bulgar khan, this
seems highly unlikely.[1] We are better informed, however, on
the splendid ceremony Justinian arranged in honor of his ally.

---

[1] For details see V. Beševliev, "K voprosu o nagrade, polučennoj
Tervelem ot Justiniana II v 705 g" ["On the Question of the Reward
Received by Tervel from Justinian II in 705"], *Vizantiiskii Vremenik* 16
(1959): 12–13.

Before a huge crowd of spectators, the emperor draped a royal cloak around the Bulgar chief's shoulders, made him sit by his side, and proclaimed him a "Caesar," while the audience knelt before them. It was the first time in the Empire's history that the title of Caesar, next in rank to the basileus himself, had been granted to a foreign prince. A number of valuable gifts—boxes full of gold and silver, weapons, and silk cloth—were then bestowed upon Tervel and his men.[2] From the Bulgars' point of view, these rewards certainly looked like tribute payment. Justinian and the Byzantine court, however, would of course prefer to look at the matter from the opposite perspective: Tervel was a caesar, a high-ranking official of the Byzantine state, ruling over his Bulgars by the emperor's grace.

There is considerable uncertainty involved in tracing the subsequent course of Byzantine-Bulgar relations during the rest of Justinian's reign. Nikephoros and Theophanes both report a brief outbreak of hostilities between Justinian and the Bulgars in about 708,[3] but it is not at all clear if the Bulgars here involved included those ruled by Tervel. While the breaking of the alliance is by no means incredible, it is rendered less likely by the fact that in 711 Tervel and Justinian were (still or again) allies, with Tervel sending troops to Justinian's aid.

Admittedly the evidence on this problem is very confused, yet it seems significant that in his account of the Bulgar-Byzantine hostilities, Nikephoros does not mention Tervel by name. Theophanes does, but it could well be that he had lost sight of the fact that there were other groups of Bulgars in Sklavinia not directly under Tervel's rule. Since it was in the Sklavinian area that Justinian encountered the foe, one possible explanation of the events of this ill-fated campaign is that

[2] On the rewarding of Tervel, see Nikephoros, p. 42; Theophanes, p. 374; also the fragmentary source materials from Suidas and *Parastaseis Syntomoi Chronikai* quoted in Beševliev, "K voprosu o nagarde, polučennoj Tervelem ot Justiniana II," pp. 8–9, along with Beševliev's commentary on them.

[3] Nikephoros, p. 43; Theophanes, p. 376. Nikephoros gives no date; Theophanes places the campaign in the third year of Justinian's second reign.

Justinian was warring against some of the Bulgars outside of Tervel's sway in a renewal of the attempt of his first reign to bring the Sklavinian lands more closely under Byzantine control.

The Proto-Bulgarian Inscriptions, which might have resolved this question, unfortunately contain a break at a crucial point and consequently only deepen the mystery. There is a clear reference in one of the inscriptions stating ". . . they broke the treaty," but the subject of this sentence is obliterated.[4] While it is possible to see this as a reference to Justinian II and thus as a confirmation of Theophanes' report, it is more likely that the treaty-breaking in question here occurred under one of the several emperors who reigned in the troubled years immediately following Justinian's death.[5]

In any event, whether it was against Tervel or other foes, Justinian's brief attempt against "the Bulgars" was disastrous. With a cavalry force under Justinian's personal command and an accompanying fleet sailing just off shore, the Byzantines proceeded along the coast of Thrace to the Bulgar stronghold of Anchialos which they captured. Soon thereafter, the Bulgars attacked and severely defeated a large band of Byzantine troops caught off guard while foraging in the area. For the next three days, Justinian and those of his men who remained in Anchialos faced the threat of a Bulgar siege, but at last they managed to escape under cover of night. Eluding the Bulgars and rejoining the Byzantine fleet, they sailed back to Constantinople in disgrace.[6]

A similar lack of military success characterized Justinian's dealings with the Arabs in his second reign, yet there are several indications that he made decided attempts to secure the good will of the new caliph Walid, the son of Abd-al-Malik. Soon after he regained the throne, the restored basileus set free about six thousand Arab prisoners of war held in custody

---

[4] Beševliev, *Die protobulgarischen Inschriften*, p. 99.

[5] For details see Beševliev, pp. 116–17; Cankova-Petkova, "Bulgarians and Byzantium," p. 44.

[6] Nikephoros, p. 43; Theophanes, p. 376.

by his predecessors.[7] Some time later, Justinian became involved in an interesting attempt to promote trade with the Caliphate and at the same time to secure the further good will of the caliph. This venture was the emperor's sending of Byzantine workers and supplies to aid in the building of the Mosque of Medina. The account of Justinian's part in this project, unmentioned by any of the Byzantine chroniclers, is preserved by two independent Arabic sources, the chronicles of al-Tabari (tenth century) and Ibn Zabala (ninth century). According to al-Tabari's report, at the caliph's request, the "Sahib al-Rum" (ruler of the Romans) sent him gold, one hundred workmen, and forty loads of mosaic cubes for the building of the "mosque of the Prophet."[8] It was the custom of scholars who dealt with this report to denounce it as fictional, until a striking confirmation of its general reliability was brought to light: an extract from Ibn Zabala's *History of Medina*, composed in that city in 814, almost a century before al-Tabari. This report quotes Walid's request to "the King of the Greeks" for aid in building the mosque. "And," Ibn Zabala continues, "he [Justinian II] sent him [Walid] loads of mosaic cubes and some twenty-odd workmen—but some say ten workmen, adding 'I have sent you ten who are equal to a hundred' —and (sent also) 80,000 dinars as a subvention for them."[9]

That the Byzantine emperor clearly expected something

---

[7] Michael the Syrian, 2:478; Gregorius Abû'l Faraj, 1:105.

[8] Al-Ṭabarî quoted in Hamilton A. R. Gibb, "Arab-Byzantine Relations under the Umayyad Caliphate," *Dumbarton Oaks Papers* 12 (1958): 225.

[9] Ibn Zabâla quoted in Gibb, "Arab-Byzantine Relations," p. 231. Theophanes, though he says nothing about these mosque-building negotiations of Walid and Justinian, does have a notice (p. 365) that Justinian in his first reign sent some columns to Abd al-Malik for building "the temple at Mecca" and that he was motivated to do so by the hope of preventing the caliph's stripping away columns from a Christian church in Jerusalem for this purpose. Gibb (p. 229) says there is no known confirmation of this report in Arabic sources. It may be that Theophanes or his source had a confused version of the Justinian-Walid negotiations, or it may be that Theophanes preserved an otherwise unknown sidelight into the Arab policy of Justinian's first reign.

in return for this aid is suggested in a relevant item from another Arabic historian. According to this report, Walid arranged to send a whole houseful of pepper, 20,000 dinars worth, to the emperor as a gift.[10]

Significantly enough, however, if Justinian hoped for establishment of a workable peace with the Caliphate, his hopes were disappointed. Even as diplomatic and commercial amenities were being exchanged between the basileus and the caliph, Arab raiders continued their periodic plundering expeditions into Byzantine territory. In about 709, a large Arab force laid siege to the fortress of Tyana in Cappadocia for nine months. The emperor sent relief troops, but many new recruits, untrained and badly disciplined, were included, and they proved to be of little assistance. Tyana at length fell to the Arabs, and emboldened by this major victory, the Arabs proceeded for the next several years to make continually deeper inroads into the Empire.[11]

What Justinian might have accomplished against the Moslem foe had his second reign lasted longer is of course impossible to say. In the loss of Tyana (and also in the previously noted disaster at Anchialos), the fact that frontier defenses were weak and the Byzantine forces poorly disciplined and poorly trained seems to have been significant in the Empire's defeat. Justinian's rash removal of the military commanders of his predecessors is almost certainly involved here. Fate had granted him the time to destroy but not to rebuild; and it would be left to a young man named Leo, who owed his rise to power to Justinian in the first place, to be Byzantium's savior from the Arab foe.

[10] Ibn Abd al-Ḥakam (a ninth-century historian) quoted in Gibb, "Arab-Byantine Relations," p. 231.

[11] On the fall of Tyana see Nikephoros, pp. 43–44; Theophanes, pp. 376–77; also al-Ṭabarî, quoted in Brooks, "The Arabs in Asia Minor," p. 192.

18

THE ADVENTURES OF LEO

IN THE spring of 705, when Justinian Rhinotmetos and Tervel's Bulgars were marching toward Constantinople, they passed through the Byzantine territory of Thrace.[1] There in a field near the side of the road, a shepherd was tending his family's flock. The young man was probably in his late teens. His name was Conon, but everyone called him Leo, for they said he was as brave as a lion. He was clever, too; though he had lived in Thrace for more than a decade and was thoroughly fluent in Greek, he still remembered the Arabic he had learned in his childhood from neighbors on the Syrian frontier.

Leo's family were some of those transplanted colonists whom Justinian II had scattered about so widely in his first reign. There was nothing to suggest that their son's future would be any different from that of thousands of Byzantine rural folk; Leo might well have passed his entire life as a Thracian sheepherder, had not Justinian and the Bulgar hosts suddenly come trooping down the road into his destiny.

Leo knew well enough the habits of hungry soldiers accustomed to living off the land; a flock of sheep was all too likely to end as a hearty barbecue, without even so much as a "by

[1] The account of the adventures of Leo is drawn from Theophanes, pp. 385–91. Bury, *Later Roman Empire*, 2:375, 381, raises the interesting conjecture that the original source of Theophanes' narrative may have been notes kept by Leo himself.

your leave" to the shepherd. No doubt with this fear in mind, Leo decided to act first. He made his way straight to Justinian himself and presented him five hundred sheep as a gift. Justinian was impressed. Impetuous as ever, he rewarded the young man with an instant commission as a *spatharius* or aide-de-camp. Thus in one giant step, Leo was able to depart from his rustic surroundings and set out on the course that would lead him at length to the Byzantine throne.

The new *spatharius* accompanied his patron to Constantinople and when Justinian was reestablished in power, continued to serve him loyally. He proved to be a very useful young officer, particularly valuable for his knowledge of Arabic. Nevertheless, because he enjoyed Justinian's favor to a high degree, Leo incurred the jealousy of some of his fellow officers, who consequently formed a conspiracy against him and charged him with plotting to take the emperor's life. On hearing these accusations, Justinian summoned Leo to stand trial, and when the evidence was presented he was pronounced innocent of the charge brought against him. This glimpse of Justinian's dealings with a suspect is in itself significant; his willingness to give the accused an apparently fair trial reveals a less arbitrary side of his nature than is disclosed elsewhere.

A short while later, however, Justinian appointed Leo to undertake an important diplomatic mission to the land of the Alans, a barbaric tribe dwelling north of the Caucasus. Leo's assignment was to enlist Alan mercenaries to invade the neighboring country of the Abasgi, an area along the eastern coast of the Black Sea which had formerly been a part of the Empire and where Justinian hoped to restore Byzantine sovereignty.[2] The emperor furnished Leo with a large sum of money for this task, and the young officer set out, depositing the money for safekeeping at the city of Phasis before crossing the Cau-

[2] Bury, *Later Roman Empire*, 2:374–75, suggests that Justinian II's ambition to bring Abasgia back under imperial control may have been motivated by the fact that it was the armies of Justinian I that had conquered Abasgia for the Empire originally.

casus into the land of the Alans. When he reached his destination and was conducting successful negotiations with the Alans
on their projected invasion of Abasgia, he was informed of a
rumor started by the chief of the Abasgi: Justinian had ordered
the withdrawal of the funds at Phasis. According to the chronicler Theophanes, who reports these happenings in detail, the
rumor was true; Justinian actually had removed the money
and was hoping thereby to secure Leo's final disappearance.
Apparently this is what Leo himself believed. It is, however,
very suspicious that Leo's source of information was the chief
of the enemy tribe whose land he was hiring the mercenaries
to invade. Such a person was scarcely likely to be a disinter-
ested reporter. Moreover, such indirect methods of ridding
himself of a foe are strikingly unlike Justinian's usual course
of action against his enemies. In any event, Leo was caught in
a difficult situation and there followed a great deal of intrigue
and counterintrigue in which his ultimate goal was to follow
through with his original assignment and coax the Alans to
invade Abasgia in spite of everything. At length, he accomplished this objective and word of his successes reached the
emperor. Justinian then made an effort to secure a safeconduct
for Leo's passage back through hostile Abasgia and his subsequent return to Constantinople. It is impossible to be certain
what the basileus had in mind here. On the surface it seems
that the offer was made in good faith, but Leo suspected
otherwise and refused to return to the capital at that time.

Nevertheless, according to Theophanes, some time later
in Justinian's reign and after a number of further adventures
Leo did return to the Byzantine capital. There is some doubt
as to the chronicler's accuracy here, and it is possible that
Leo's return did not take place until the reign of Anastasius II
(713–715).[3] If, however, Theophanes is correct and Leo did

[3] The later Byzantine chronicler Zonaras, in his retelling of Theophanes' story, states categorically that Leo did not return to Constantinople
until the reign of Anastasius II. Perhaps Zonaras merely felt that Leo's
return in Justinian's lifetime was altogether incongruous with the emper-
or's reputed ill will toward him or perhaps he actually had access to more
accurate data at this point. For details see Bury, *Later Roman Empire*,
2:395.

return to the Byzantine court while Justinian was still alive, Justinian took no action against him. This is a clue, though admittedly only a conjectural one, that would indicate that Leo's fears about the emperor's ill will toward him were groundless from the start.

Nevertheless, whether Justinian had plotted against him or not, Leo seems to have believed that he did. Leo's known antipathies, in turn, very likely would have colored the works of chroniclers—the "lost sources" of Theophanes—which may have been written during his reign. We have here, in short, an intriguing hypothesis to explain the growth of a "black legend" against Justinian II, an explanation of why Theophanes describes him in so much harsher terms than does Nikephoros. It must be emphasized that it is only a theory; there is no positive proof. Yet the circumstantial evidence is so strong that it can scarcely be ignored. Leo III may have had valid reason to hate Justinian. Yet it is ironic that this one-time shepherd of Thrace, Justinian's protégé turned enemy, likely had so great a role in moulding for ill the whole subsequent historical reputation of the man who started him on the road to fame and fortune.

19

COMPROMISE WITH THE PAPACY

JUSTINIAN'S quest for allies in his second reign led him, as we have seen, to cultivate the good will of his powerful eastern neighbors: Khazars, Bulgars, and Arabs. To the west lay another force to be reckoned with: the papacy. Here Justinian's diplomacy would lead to a happy conclusion, probably the most constructive accomplishment of his second term as emperor. Because, however, the Byzantine chroniclers Nikephoros and Theophanes were almost altogether unconcerned about Western affairs, they have nothing to report on this subject. Fortunately, the excellent Western source, the *Liber Pontificalis*, helps to fill the gap.[1]

The anonymous author of the *Liber Pontificalis*, as we have seen, wrote almost contemporaneously with the events he described. It was he who preserved the details of the vigorous squabble between Justinian and Pope Sergius, ended only by the emperor's deposition in 695. With his restoration to the throne ten years later ("immediately as he entered his palace," as the papal chronicler puts it), Justinian was determined to reopen the whole question of the Quinisext Canons. Pope Sergius was dead by now, and the reigning pontiff was John VII, whose mosaic portrait is still preserved in the Holy

[1] *Liber Pontificalis*, 1:385–91. Good secondary-source background is to be found in Fliche and Martin, *Histoire de l'Église*, 5:198–200; Görres, "Justinian II und das römische Papsttum," pp. 451–53; Hodgkin, *Italy and Her Invaders*, 6:369–78.

Crypt in the Vatican. Pope John was a Greek, learned and eloquent, according to the *Liber Pontificalis*, but characterized by an unusually timid disposition. To him Justinian sent two metropolitan bishops with the controversial Tomes containing the text of the Quinisext enactments. They also carried a *sacra* (imperial letter) in which Justinian requested that the pope convene a synod and there approve the canons acceptable to him while rejecting the others.

It is significant in light of the subsequent course of events that at this point in his narrative, the author of the *Liber Pontificalis* is himself adamantly opposed to the Quinisext Canons, "in which were written diverse chapters contrary to the Roman Church." Had the papacy accepted the canons *in toto* soon thereafter, it is most unlikely that such a remark as this would be found in the official papal history.

In spite of the seeming reasonableness of the emperor's message, Pope John apparently feared to trust Justinian and sent the Tomes back to him, "emending them not at all" but refusing to grant his assent. This course of action the papal biographer, with an unusual tone of criticism, describes as dictated by John's "human frailty." Before the emperor had time to exert further pressure on Pope John, the pontiff died (in 707) and Rome faced the problem of selecting a successor. Early in 708, the new pope Sisinnius, an elderly and ailing Syrian, took office but lived only twenty days thereafter. His successor was another Syrian, Constantine, "a very mild man," who, as the subsequent course of events will reveal, proved able to work exceedingly well with Justinian II.

It is tempting to see, throughout the crisis of the papal succession in 708, the possible activity of imperial agents on the scene in Rome to assure that a pope was chosen who would be likely to cooperate with the emperor.[2] Such a conjecture could explain the choice of the invalid Sisinnius, who presumably would be too weak to raise much protest to the emperor's wishes. The fact that both Sisinnius and Constan-

---

[2] So suggests Mann, *Lives of the Popes*, vol. 1, pt. 2, p. 126, although he does not elaborate on the question.

tine were easterners, Syrians, is significant, too, for as such they were less likely to find anything offensive in the Quinisext canons than a Western European would have been. Also thought-provoking is Pope Constantine's name. Almost certainly he had been born either during the reign of Justinian's father Constantine IV or his grandfather Constantine III and named for the reigning emperor. Although of course there must have been many children baptized Constantine whose families had no ties with the imperial court, neither is it inconceivable that Pope Constantine owed his name to family connections with the Byzantine imperial dynasty.

Whatever role Justinian may have played in Pope Constantine's election, however, the new pontiff clearly was determined to be more than a mere puppet in the emperor's hands. This is evidenced by the fact that in 710, the question of the Quinisext Canons was still unresolved. Finally in October of that year, Pope Constantine and a large party of clerics, in compliance with an imperial invitation, embarked on a journey to the eastern court. Because of the onset of cold weather, they tarried rather long in Naples and Sicily and at other points along the way, and it would take them several months to reach their destination. Instructions went out from Justinian to all his officials along the papal route that the pope was to be accorded the same respect they would show to the basileus himself. The *Liber Pontificalis* specifically mentions the reception the papal party received at one point in their journey from Theophilos, patrician and strategos of the Karabisianoi. This man was very likely Theophilos of Cherson, one of the volunteers who had sailed with Justinian to recover his throne and who was now enjoying the reward for his service.[3]

It was probably in the early spring of 711 that Constantine and his party reached Constantinople. At the seventh milestone outside the city, they were met by a delegation of patricians and clergy, headed by Justinian's little son, the Co-Emperor Tiberius (now six years old) and the Patriarch Cyrus

---

[3] *Liber Pontificalis*, 1:390. See also Antoniadis-Bibicou, *Études d'histoire maritime*, p. 64.

of Constantinople. All were mounted on horses decked with the most lavish accoutrements, "imperial" saddles, gilded bridles, and saddle cloths of rich fabric. Great crowds of people "all rejoicing and holding a holiday" swarmed out from the city to join the festivities and accompany the triumphal procession into the city. Probably the papal party entered the capital through the Golden Gate,[4] used only for great ceremonial occasions, and then proceeded along the Mesé (Middle Street) to Placidia Palace, the residence customarily used to house dignitaries from the papal court.

Justinian himself was not present for the pope's arrival in Constantinople; he was in Nicaea. But when he heard that Constantine had reached the capital, the *Liber Pontificalis* reports, the emperor was "full of great joy" and sent him a *sacra*, arranging to meet him soon in Nicomedia. The subsequent meeting of the pope and the basileus was marked by splendid ceremony. Justinian, crown on head, bowed to kiss the pope's feet; the pope and Justinian then embraced each other as brothers. "And great was the joy of the people, all perceiving such great humility on the part of the good prince." The following Sunday, Constantine celebrated Mass; the emperor received communion from the pope's hands and asked him to pray for pardon for his sins.

While the author of the *Liber Pontificalis* describes the pageantry of Pope Constantine's eastern visit in detail, he has far less to relate on the subject of the Quinisext Canons. It is clear, however, that the emperor and the papal delegation held a conference and reached an agreement acceptable to both sides. In all likelihood, Constantine assented to most of the canons and was released from the obligation to accept the few that seemed so objectionable to Rome.[5] Much of the credit for the success of these negotiations probably belongs to the deacon Gregory (later to be Pope Gregory II) who when "questioned by the Prince Justinian concerning certain chap-

[4] Fliche and Martin, *Histoire de l'Église*, p. 199.
[5] Especially canon 36. See Görres, "Justinian II und das römische Papsttum," p. 453.

ters, made the best response and solved every problem."[6] Although some historians have doubted that the strong-willed Justinian would have ever agreed to a compromise, the weight of evidence indicates that he did. There is no known copy of the Quinisext Canons bearing a notice of papal ratification.[7] The English scholar Bede, who completed his world chronicle a few years after the pope's visit to Byzantium, speaks of the Quinisext Council as *erratica*,[8] which he scarcely would have done had the entire collection of the canons gained papal approval; and there is, too, the previously mentioned condemnatory note on the canons in the *Liber Pontificalis* itself, in the chapter on Pope John VII. Clearly, Justinian II realized the futility of attempting to force the canons *in toto* on the Western church and, heeding the reasoned arguments of the deacon Gregory, agreed to some modifications. Justinian's further good will toward the papacy is suggested in the notice in the *Liber Pontificalis* that he "renewed all the privileges of the Church,"[9] though it is not certain exactly what this means.

In any event, Justinian's willingness to work for peaceful compromise and his apparent yielding to the pope on some of their points of disagreement scarcely accord with the course of unreasoned action that the hostile Byzantine chroniclers would lead us to expect from him. Rather, in his dealings with the papacy throughout his second reign, Justinian appears as a responsible, clear-headed sovereign, determined to undo some of the harm caused by the mistakes of his earlier years.

[6] *Liber Pontificalis*, 1:396.
[7] Hefele, *Councils*, 5:242.
[8] Bede, *De Sex Aetatibus*, p. 316.
[9] *Liber Pontificalis*, 1:391.

20

JUSTINIAN AND RAVENNA:

A MATTER OF MOTIVE

Thus far, it may be noticed, most of the significant indications of constructive statesmanship in Justinian's second reign come from non-Byzantine sources. It is from Arab historians that we learn of his diplomatic relations with the Caliph Walid, and from the Roman author of the *Liber Pontificalis* that we gather the details of his dealings with the papacy. Nevertheless, it is also a non-Byzantine source, the ninth-century chronicle of Agnellus of Ravenna, that provides one of the most serious charges against him.[1] Agnellus describes Justinian's attack on the capital city of the Italian exarchate as based upon the emperor's desire for revenge; certain citizens of Ravenna had played an important role in inflicting *rhinokopia* upon him, and now all Ravenna must pay. Agnellus's characterization of Justinian is, in fact, very similar to that of Nikephoros and Theophanes, though neither of them has anything to report of this particular crisis.

That an imperial attack on Ravenna took place during Justinian's second reign is confirmed by the independent testimony of the *Liber Pontificalis*.[2] It is indisputable that Justin-

[1] Agnellus, pp. 366–71.
[2] *Liber Pontificalis*, 1:389–90.

ian undertook extremely harsh and ultimately unwise action
against the unfortunate city. The question is why? and here,
fortunately, the *Liber Pontificalis* contains insights which the
later chronicler Agnellus neglected to mention and which
reveal Justinian's action to have been based on more substantial grounds than Agnellus's alleged revenge motive.

As the *Liber Pontificalis* clearly shows, the emperor's dealings with Rome and Ravenna were closely interwoven. Not
long after Pope Constantine took office in 708, the new Archbishop of Ravenna, Felix, became involved in a serious squabble with the papacy. The rivalry between Rome and Ravenna
was a matter of long standing that more than once had
erupted into open violence in years past. At the core of the
matter was Ravenna's local pride as capital of the Exarchate
of Italy and accompanying resentment over the fact that
Ravenna's archbishop had to swear obedience to the pope.
For about thirty years before Pope Constantine took office,
tensions between the two cities had lain dormant. Now with
the ordination of Archbishop Felix the old crisis broke out
afresh, for once ordained Felix refused to assent to a document
prescribed by the pope in which he was supposed to promise
to do nothing contrary to the unity of the Church or the safety
of the Empire. It is significant that the leaders of Ravenna's
local government supported Felix in this refusal. Revolutionary
activity was clearly in the wind in Ravenna.[3]

Eventually, Archbishop Felix produced his own version of
the controversial document and sent it to Rome, but Pope
Constantine was not satisfied. It was at this juncture that
Justinian II entered the controversy, dispatching a fleet to
Ravenna where his agents would attempt, through vigorous
and violent tactics, to teach the city a lesson. From the order
of events narrated by the author of the *Liber Pontificalis*, it
seems clear that the emperor's expedition against Ravenna
was occasioned by the obvious signs of unrest emanating from

---

[3] *Liber Pontificalis*, 1:389. See also Hodgkin, *Italy and Her Invaders*,
6:371–72; Charles Diehl, *Études sur l'administration byzantine dans
l'exarchat de Ravenne* (Paris, 1888; reprint ed., New York, 1959), p. 361.

the city, particularly Archbishop Felix's opposition to the pope. In view of the way his own relations with the papacy were progressing by this time (709), Justinian may well have felt that Felix's opposition was a challenge to himself as well as to the pope. He may have felt, too, that by sending imperial troops against Ravenna he would be doing the pope such a favor that Constantine would be obliged to cooperate more fully on the Quinisext Canons. There is a definite air of intrigue in the details that the papal chronicler omits to mention, and although it is not necessary to blame the "very mild" Constantine personally for Justinian's methods, the *Liber Pontificalis* leaves no doubt that Rome considered the emperor's blows against Ravenna just punishment for "those who were disobedient to the apostolic see."[4]

The chronicler Agnellus, who provides the only other independent account of Justinian's activities against Ravenna, wrote about a century later. His sources are unknown; it is not impossible that the *Liber Pontificalis* was among them, but his interpretation of Justinian is very different from that of the papal biographer. According to Agnellus, the emperor's fury against Ravenna was a direct result of the part that certain of its citizens had played in his mutilation. Although there is apparently no evidence elsewhere that people of Ravenna had any part in this deed, it is easy to see how such an explanation would commend itself to popular rumor; the fact that he had suffered *rhinokopia* and lived to reign again was the most memorable thing about the Emperor Justinian II.

With lively imagination and frequent echoes of Vergil's *Aeneid*, Agnellus describes how Justinian lay awake night after night, wondering what to do about Ravenna and how at last he determined upon a crafty plot. Agnellus's tale, apart from its emphasis on the revenge motive, may well be largely authentic.[5] Living in Ravenna himself, Agnellus probably had

[4] *Liber Pontificalis*, 1:389.

[5] It is likely that Agnellus had access to documents in the ecclesiastical archives of Ravenna. For details see Fliche and Martin, *Histoire de l'Église*, 5:9.

access to good sources; moreover, much of the story is in general accord with the data in the *Liber Pontificalis*. The narrative may be summarized briefly. Justinian sent a fleet to Ravenna, having instructed the officer in command (the patrician Theodore, according to the *Liber Pontificalis*) to hold a great outdoor banquet for the local dignitaries. Then when these men arrived, they were conducted according to plan inside the commander's tent, where they were seized and bound, to be hauled off to Constantinople. Among them was Archbishop Felix. The imperial troops then entered the city pillaging and burning.

Some time thereafter the prisoners from Ravenna reached the imperial capital and were brought before the emperor with the golden nose. Agnellus, whose writing is full of vivid details, describes Justinian seated upon a gold and emerald throne and wearing a headdress of gold and pearls fashioned for him by his empress. The emperor's plan was to put all the captives from Ravenna to death, but, Agnellus continues, a vision appeared to him in the night, imploring him to spare Archbishop Felix. This he promised to do, and although the others were put to death by various gruesome means, Felix's sentence was reduced to the "merciful" penalty of blinding. Agnellus describes the method: a silver dish was heated to incandescence and filled with vinegar, and Felix was forced to stare directly at it until his sight was destroyed. He was then banished to "Pontus," on the coast of the Black Sea.

That Ravenna did not submit tamely to these blows is clear from Agnellus's subsequent narrative, although the actual course of the rebellion which broke out there is very obscure. Agnellus directs most of his attention to narrating the rousing speeches (full of Vergilian quotations) of the rebel leader. The uncertainty of the events in Ravenna is increased by a notice in the *Liber Pontificalis* which has no parallel in Agnellus's account. The papal biographer reports that in 710 Pope Constantine, by this time on his way to visit the emperor in the East, met the new imperial exarch, John Rizocopus, at Naples, where the two exchanged polite civilities. The exarch then proceeded to Rome, where for reasons unspecified, he executed four papal officials, and finally to Ravenna where "for his very evil deeds he died a most shameful death by the judgment of God."[6] It is not at all clear whose side Rizocopus was on in this struggle. One possibility is that he was fulfilling the emperor's orders in executing the papal officials and that he met his "most shameful death" at the hands of the Ravenna rebels. This explanation, however, is by no means certain. In light of the flourishing good will between Justinian and Pope Constantine at this point, it is difficult to see why the emperor would have desired the removal of the papal officials. On the other hand, the Ravenna rebels were clearly opposed to both pope and emperor and probably would have had much more to gain by the execution of these men. It could well be that Rizocopus had thrown in his lot with the revolutionaries in the capital of the exarchate. Further support for this view is to be had from the fact that the author of the *Liber Pontificalis* speaks of the death of the exarch and those of the Ravenna citizens previously executed by Justinian in very similar language; both instances are in accord with the just judgment of God. Notable, too, is the fact that the *Liber Pontificalis* clearly does not say that Rizocopus was killed; indeed the fact that his death is described as *turpissima* may hint that it was rather the result of some foul disease.

In any case, whatever role the exarch played in the Ravenna uprising, the struggle there against the imperial government went on. It would still be in progress when Justinian died more than a year later.

[6] *Liber Pontificalis*, 1:390.

21

THE CHERSON CRISIS

I N EXAMINING the report of
Agnellus that Justinian acted against Ravenna solely out of
revenge, we are fortunate in possessing the counterevidence
from the *Liber Pontificalis* that shows the emperor concerned
to crush the revolutionary activity of Ravenna's Archbishop
Felix and his adherents. In turning to Cherson, the other city
reputedly chastized by Justinian's vengefulness, we possess no
such independent testimony. To understand what went on
there, we have almost nothing but the chronicles of Nikephoros and Theophanes, and any attempt to evaluate the data
they present must be based to a large extent on what the
chroniclers themselves actually say and how well their reports
hold up in the face of critical analysis. Their accounts, which
are very similar, are almost certainly based on the lost "713
Chronicle." This nearness to the date of the happenings described probably means that their narratives of the course of
events are largely reliable. But their explanation of the reasons
underlying Justinian's policy almost surely contain items from
the propaganda of his successor, Philippikos Vardan.

The key to the whole of the Cherson crisis is that of the
emperor's motive. According to the chroniclers, he was acti-
vated solely by his hatred of the city that had tried to betray
him to Tiberius Apsimar when he was living in exile there.
But there are several significant indications that the desire for

vengeance, even if it played a part in the emperor's action, was not his only or even his major reason for moving against Cherson. If he had been motivated solely by vengefulness, it is very odd that he waited more than five years after regaining his throne before taking action against Cherson. Moreover, as the chroniclers themselves reveal (though they do not enlarge upon the subject), Justinian's unreliable brother-in-law the khagan had recently set up in Cherson a Khazar governor known as the *tudun*.[1] This encroachment in the Byzantine sphere of influence was enough to give Justinian a very valid cause for alarm. Finally, as has been noted, the chroniclers' information is probably derived from the "713 Chronicle," which on the subject of Justinian's fall must have reflected propaganda current immediately thereafter. Justinian's successor, Philippikos Vardan, naturally would not present the khagan in the light of an enemy of Byzantium since it was largely thanks to him that Philippikos had gained the throne. Yet in all likelihood, the khagan's expansionist ambition was indeed the crucial factor in setting into action Justinian's expeditions against Cherson.

It was early in 711 that the emperor dispatched to Cherson an army that, according to the chroniclers, numbered 100,000 men and was under the command of Stephen Asmiktos.[2] This was very likely the same Stephen of Cherson who had accompanied Justinian on his flight to the Bulgars a few years earlier. Stephen carried orders to reduce the area around Cherson and Bosporus and to slay "all" the inhabitants in the area. A certain officer, Helias, was then to be appointed

[1] Some editors of the chroniclers mistakenly took *Tudun* as a proper name. Dunlop, *Khazars*, p. 174, shows that it was an official Khazar title. That the tudun had not been installed in Cherson for any length of time is indicated by the fact that when the exiled Justinian wished to contact the Khazars, it was necessary for him to go to Doros to do so. See also Minns, *Scythians and Greeks*, pp. 542–43.

[2] The chronicle sources for the Cherson crisis are Nikephoros, pp. 44–48; Theophanes, pp. 377–81. Most historians accept them verbatim; very few are as skeptical as Minns, *Scythians and Greeks*, p. 532, who remarks: "The accounts of his [Justinian's] vengeance are just a string of legends which leave us quite in the dark as to his real motives."

governor. The mention of Bosporus, a city under Khazar control, is a further clue that the expedition was largely directed against the khagan. As for the reputed order to slay all the inhabitants, it is manifestly absurd; if Cherson were to be wiped off the face of the map, what need would there be for a governor?

The chroniclers' narratives continue with the emperor's troops apparently accomplishing the subjugation of Cherson with success. Aside from the casualties of the actual conquest, the Patriarch Nikephoros reports that Stephen had seven of the leading citizens executed by roasting; an unspecified number of others were drowned, and a group of about thirty men, including Zoïlos, the "chief of the citizens," and the Khazar *tudun* were shipped off to Constantinople along with their families. Apparently Nikephoros is correct in stating that they were imprisoned there. Theophanes, whose text is very corrupt at this point, appears to say that Zoïlos and the *tudun* were executed, but this has to be a mistake in view of their subsequent return to Cherson.[3] A number of youths were also collected who were to be sold into slavery.

Justinian reportedly was displeased with the way things were being done, and particularly over the matter of the youths reserved for slavery. Therefore, he ordered that the youths be sent to Constantinople at once. His officers in Cherson had no choice but to obey his command, though the October weather was not conducive to sea travel. A storm arose, the whole fleet was destroyed, and about 73,000 lives were lost. Justinian, the chroniclers allege, received this news with pleasure.[4] This report contains several suspiciously illogical features. The emperor's reputed joy at the sinking of the fleet has every mark of anti-Justinian propaganda; regardless of how he felt about Chersonites or Khazars, it appears incredible that he would have rejoiced over the loss of a number of his own troops and ships. The reliability of the great number of reported losses is also questionable; yet even if due allow-

---

[3] For further detail see Hodgkin, *Italy and Her Invaders*, 6:380.

[4] Nikephoros, p. 45; Theophanes, p. 378.

ance is made for exaggeration here, one may wonder why it was necessary for such a substantial part of the Byzantine force to be departing from Cherson with the captives. Surely the number of captives itself cannot have been very large, for as the subsequent course of events reveals, Cherson remained full of Chersonites. It is tempting to speculate on the possibility that Justinian was actually ordering the withdrawal of the major part of the expedition, with a view to bringing the Cherson campaign to a close.

In any case, for reasons unspecified, Justinian soon decided that he was not satisfied with the situation as it stood in Cherson, and according to Nikephoros he began making plans to dispatch another fleet against the city. Theophanes says that the fleet was actually sent, but since this information is not in accord with the other details he and Nikephoros both present, it is generally conceded to be a mistake.[5] Both chroniclers indicate that the emperor desired further vengeance, but they also report that the Chersonites sent an appeal to the khagan for additional aid and that Khazar troops arrived to help defend the city. It is certainly debatable which side was more eager to intensify hostilities at this juncture. Then (probably thanks to Khazar encouragement) the Byzantine troops from the first expedition remaining in Cherson under the command of Helias were convinced to throw in their lot with the Chersonites and their Khazar allies. When he received word of this, Justinian determined upon a sudden change of policy. He released Zoïlos and the Khazar *tudun* and sent them back to Cherson with a small Byzantine troop of about three hundred men. There they were to attempt to restore the status quo as far as possible and were specifically ordered to convey Justinian's apologies to the khagan. Helias was to be arrested and sent back to Byzantium.

Justinian's attempt to restore order came too late. The Chersonites at first refused to deal with his envoys; then, pretending to change their attitude, they invited Justinian's men into the city and immediately put to death the leaders. The

---

[5] Breckenridge, *Numismatic Iconography*, p. 16.

remainder were seized and sent off to Khazaria along with
Zoïlos and the *tudun*. On this journey the *tudun* died, and
according to what was apparently a Khazar custom, the three
hundred Byzantine captives with him were slain to accompany
him to the next world.[6]

For the rebels at Cherson, the next logical step was
providing their cause with a rival contender for the imperial
title, and an Armenian officer named Vardan, who had accompanied Helias on the first expedition, was accorded this
dangerous privilege. Some years earlier, Vardan had been
imprisoned by Tiberius Apsimar for imperial pretensions, and
more recently released by Justinian and promoted to high rank
in the imperial army. He seems to have been an easy-going,
popular officer, with a reputation for mildness. He was a Monothelete heretic, but this apparently did not bother anyone at
the time. Assuming the properly classical name Philippikos,
which he felt more suited to the dignity of Empire than the
Armenian Vardan, he was proclaimed basileus.

When Justinian heard of these developments he was fur-
ious, and according to our sources took drastic vengeance
upon Helias's family in Constantinople.[7] There is no way of
proving or disproving these charges. In any case, once Justinian was fully aware of the seriousness of the situation in Cherson, he proceeded to send another expedition against the city,
this one headed by a certain Mauros. The Byzantine troops
arrived and set up siege. Just as the situation was beginning to
look hopeless for the rebels, further aid arrived from the Khazars. Justinian's forces, who dared not return to their master
in defeat, switched their allegiance to Philippikos Vardan,
although Vardan himself, uncertain of the outcome, had left
Cherson and taken refuge at the court of the khagan.

When Justinian received no news from Cherson, he made
the serious tactical error of leaving Constantinople and proceeding with his army and auxiliaries furnished by his Bulgarian ally Tervel to Damatrys in Asia Minor. At this same time,

---

[6] Nikephoros, p. 46; Theophanes, p. 379.
[7] Nikephoros, p. 46; Theophanes, p. 379.

FIGURE 12
Philippikos Vardan; coin of his reign, 711–713
Dumbarton Oaks Collection

rebellion against the Byzantine government, sparked by the
Arabs, was raging in Armenia.[8] Since Philippikos Vardan was
himself an Armenian, Justinian may have thought these troubles were part of a connected plot and that the rival claimant
to the throne would attempt to coordinate efforts with the
rebels in his home area.[9] If so, the emperor's entry into Asia
Minor is certainly more understandable. But as events turned
out, when Vardan left the Khazar court, he rejoined the fleet
at Cherson and from there sailed straightway to Constanti-

[8] Ghévond, p. 34. Significantly, Justinian retaliated against the
Armenian rebels only by having the Patriarch Cyrus place them under
anathema.
[9] So suggests Breckenridge, *Numismatic Iconography*, p. 16.

nople. When Justinian learned of this, he turned back toward the capital, "roaring like a lion," Theophanes says. It was too late; the city had fallen to the new emperor Philippikos without a battle. Justinian then tried to get back to his camp at Damatrys, but at the twelfth milestone outside Constantinople, he was overtaken by a band of troops under command of Helias. They carried an offer of general amnesty from Philippikos for all who would desert the *Rhinotmetos*. Only a few of Justinian's officers would remain faithful to him to the death. The chroniclers give particular notice to Barasbakurios, one of Justinian's original Chersonite followers, who now held the titles of protopatrician and count of the Opsikion theme, and whom Vardan's agents tracked down and slew. Justinian's cause was obviously lost.

Helias reserved for himself the privilege of slaying his enemy. Reportedly he struck off the fallen emperor's head with one blow, then forwarded this grim trophy to Philippikos Vardan. According to a Byzantine *Necrologium* recording vital statistics on the various emperors' deaths, the date of Justinian's execution was November 4, 711. He was forty-two years old. His victorious foes refused to accord him the dignity of Christian burial, and his headless corpse was tossed into the sea.[10]

Meanwhile, Philippikos forwarded Justinian's head to Rome and Ravenna for public display. Reputedly there was much glee in Ravenna over Justinian's death. Agnellus tells, for instance, of a woman, sister of one of the Ravenna rebels whom Justinian had executed, who had often declared she would die happy if only she could live to see the emperor's fall. When Justinian's head was paraded through the streets of the town, she stared out her window long and hard, thanked God, and fell over dead—and presumably happy.[11] In Rome, however, where the papal party was his ally, there were those who mourned Justinian's fall. The author of the *Liber Pontificalis*, writing soon after the event, sorrowfully noted the "mel-

---

[10] Grierson, "The Tombs and Obits of the Byzantine Emperors," pp. 50–51.

[11] Agnellus, p. 371.

ancholy tidings that Justinian, the most Christian and orthodox Emperor, was murdered."[12] The fact that his successor was the heretic Philippikos no doubt enhanced Justinian's reputation in the eyes of the papal historian, but this does not necessarily negate the sincerity of the dismay felt in Rome when the city learned of his death.

A tragic epilogue to the history of Justinian II is the fate of his little son.[13] When Justinian's mother, Anastasia, received news of his death, she took six-year-old Tiberius to the church of the Virgin of Blachernae where she hoped they might find sanctuary. Two agents of Philippikos Vardan, Mauros (who had led the third expedition to Cherson) and John called Strouthos ("the Sparrow"), entered. Anastasia fell on her knees before them pleading tearfully that Tiberius's life be spared. The boy meanwhile clung fast to the altar with one hand; in the other he grasped some fragments of the True Cross. About his neck hung a reliquary full of valuable holy objects.[14] While Mauros stood detained by Anastasia's pleas, his companion moved on to the altar and seized the little emperor. Strouthos placed the True Cross fragments upon the altar and transferred the reliquary from the boy's neck to his own. Then he carried Tiberius outside to the porch of a nearby church. There the son of Justinian II was stripped of his clothing and slaughtered "like a sheep." The house of Heraclius had been wiped from the face of the earth.

There are still a number of intriguing questions about Justinian's family that remain unanswered. So far as we know, no harm befell his mother, Anastasia. It was not the usual Byzantine practice to punish women for the sins of their menfolk, though if she followed the precedent of many other impe-

[12] *Liber Pontificalis*, 1:391. News of Justinian's death reached Rome in January, 712.

[13] Described in Nikephoros, pp. 47–48; Theophanes, p. 380.

[14] The trust of Tiberius and his grandmother in these holy relics to aid them is a *locus classicus* for typical Byzantine belief in the efficacy of such relics in the pre-iconoclastic period. For details, see H. J. Magoulias, "The Lives of Byzantine Saints as Sources for the History of Magic," *Byzantion* 38 (1967): 251.

rial ladies, Anastasia probably entered a convent when her family had fallen from power. How long she lived we are given no hint, but ultimately she would receive honorable burial in the same tomb with Constantine IV, the husband of her youth.[15]

Concerning Theodora of the Khazars, we know even less. Because there is no mention of her in the chroniclers' accounts of Justinian's fall and because it was Anastasia, the grandmother, who tried in vain to save little Tiberius, many have assumed that Theodora was already dead. But we have no record of her receiving a suitably imperial burial, as she certainly would have had she predeceased her husband. Perhaps, then, she was with Justinian in his last days, and perhaps in time Vardan returned her to her brother Ibouzeros. These are only conjectures, however, and all we can say with certainty is that the Khazar lady simply disappears from history.

[15] Grierson, "Tombs and Obits of the Byzantine Emperors," p. 32.

22

CONCLUSION

THE time has come to tie the pieces together. Justinian II of Byzantium lived and died, and with the passing of time became the subject of intensified historiographical hostility from men of his own empire. Then as more centuries passed, his memory slipped into oblivion. It has been our object to rescue him from that oblivion and, moreover, while examining his place in history, to vindicate him from some of the charges launched against him by his historiographical adversaries. We may ask now if the effort is worthwhile. Granted that Justinian's life story contains a saga of strange adventure, a tale so unlikely that were it invented by a writer of fiction it would be denounced as incredible. To know that such things could and did happen is to bring us closer to the world of the early Byzantine Empire.

Yet over and beyond the intrinsic interest of the tale of the emperor-who-lost-his-nose is the matter of Justinian's real importance in the history of Byzantium. It might of course be said at the outset that any man who was for sixteen years head of state of one of the greatest world powers of his time merits some attention from historians. With further probing into Justinian's accomplishments, we find that his efforts in dealing with administrative, religious, diplomatic, and military problems reveal him as a man of energy and determination and not without considerable ability. His concern for furthering

the development of the themes and for the founding of strategically located military colonies shows how he attempted to
strengthen the Empire's defenses; and the survival of some of
his colonies for many years thereafter reveals the soundness
of his planning. His often aggressive military policies were not
always wise, but neither were they always disastrous. Particularly in the Sklavinian campaign of his first reign he made substantial gains in rebuilding the Empire's position in an area
where barbarians had made deep inroads. Nor was Justinian unskilled in the amenities of peaceable diplomacy, as is
revealed in such diverse incidents as his sending aid for the
caliph's mosque-building project and his harmonious relations
with Pope Constantine. In the area of church polity, Justinian's Quinisext Canons (in spite of their cool reception by the
papacy) were accepted by the Eastern church as the work of
an ecumenical council and were respected accordingly. In the
realm of administration, the *Nomos Georgikos* (if indeed it is
Justinian's work) reveals the emperor's concern for safeguard-
ing the rights of the free farmer class. It offers, too, a major
hint that he may well have been responsible for the Byzantine
tax reform that aided the small landholders to escape bondage
to the soil. The emerging picture of Justinian's rule thus indicates much that is constructive in his work, quite apart from
the more unfortunate aspects of his reigns which the chronicle
sources emphasize and often exaggerate.

There is much in Justinian's life and in the conditions of
the Empire under his rule that might be described as typically
Byzantine. Yet while Justinian II belongs to a particular state,
it is important to recall, too, that he belongs to a particular
historical era, one in which important changes were taking
place. Through study of the Empire under Justinian II, one
may derive much insight into the early medieval world in the
midst of transition. Justinian was "Emperor of the Romans,"
and his contacts with the cities of Ravenna and Old Rome are
evidence that he had by no means lost interest in the West.
Yet the Empire, even as he ruled over it, was coming more
and more to face east. A number of the features that would
contribute to the distinctive character of medieval Byzantium

are present under Justinian II's rule. The growing differences between Eastern and Western Christianity, the imperial efforts to protect small landholders and insure against the rise of an overmighty aristocracy, the continuing development of the themes, and the pressures of friendly and hostile relations with other Eastern powers are important not only in the context of Justinian's own time but as symptomatic of the future course of the Empire's development.

Differences between Latin and Greek Christianity would accelerate rapidly in the century after Justinian's fall. It is indicative of the growing coolness between Constantinople and Rome that Pope Constantine's visit to Justinian II in 711 marks the last time in history that a Roman pontiff journeyed to the Eastern court. The iconoclastic upheaval brought about by the Emperor Leo III added considerably to East-West tensions, and in the reign of his son, Constantine V, the city of Ravenna would slip from Byzantine control. Popes would turn more and more for support to the rising kingdom of the Franks, until finally in A.D. 800 a pope would crown the Frankish monarch Charlemagne as Roman emperor. Byzantium's claim to sole emperorship over Christendom hereafter would meet many a formidable challenge from Western Europe.

Within the Byzantine state, the hints of Justinian II's concern to protect the small free farmer class from absorption by an overmighty aristocracy find fulfillment in the work of some of the later emperors. An independent small-landowner class did survive for centuries in the Byzantine world, though the land hungry ambitions of the great nobles continued to prove a vexing problem for many of the Byzantine sovereigns. It is not until we reach the reigns of Romanos Lekapenos (920–944) and then of his great-grandson, Basil II (976–1025) that we find emperors whose legislation provided a genuinely effective curtailment of the growth of large landed estates at the expense of impoverished freeholders.

The theme system, so closely associated in its origins with the entire Heraclian dynasty, was maintained and expanded by the emperors of the eighth, ninth, and tenth centuries. As Justinian II and his ancestors had foreseen, this combination

of civil and military governorship in the hands of strategoi provided what was probably the most workable form of government for the Byzantine provinces, while the thematic armies
proved invaluable in maintaining frontier defenses. Justinian
II's own lifetime and particularly his second reign were marked
by a grave Arab crisis, and the emperor is justly to be criti-
cized for his failure to strengthen frontier defenses after his
return to the imperial throne. The Byzantine state, however,
would begin a period of military recovery with Leo III's great
victory in 717/18 over the Arab besiegers of Constantinople.
The darkest hour passed, and though the Arabs would remain
a formidable foe of Byzantium for a long time to come, by the
ninth and tenth centuries we find the Byzantine armies of the
themes taking the offensive and recovering at least some of
the Empire's lost territories in Asia Minor and Syria.

The Balkan area, where Justinian II had battled the Sklavinians and the Bulgars, was destined to remain a crucial
territory in Byzantium's maintenance of the balance of power
vis à vis her barbarian neighbors. Over the course of generations, many Slavs were absorbed into Byzantine civilization;
the Byzantine missionary efforts among them, particularly
from the ninth century onward, played a large role in this
outcome. But while some of the Slavic peoples became inte-
grated into the Byzantine state, the Bulgars, who evolved eth-
nically into a mixture of old Bulgar and Slavic stock, remained
almost continually Byzantium's foe and most dangerous rival
for ascendancy in the Balkans. Many of the emperors of the
iconoclastic epoch, and later on, of the great Macedonian
dynasty, warred against the Bulgars and crushed them tempo-
rarily, while very few found it expedient to imitate the cultiva-
tion of their good will exemplified by the alliance of Justinian
II and Tervel. Finally, Basil II, the "Bulgar-slayer," in the
early eleventh century would deliver the knock-out blow to
the independence of the old Bulgarian kingdom and annex it
securely to the Byzantine realm.

In Justinian II's lifetime, few could have foreseen the
greatness and surprising resiliency of the medieval Byzantine
Empire as it was destined to develop, though many of the

facets of the Empire's development are in some way foreshadowed in his reign. Better times did not arrive immediately with Justinian's fall in 711. Philippikos Vardan's reign was short and disastrous. Among other woes came news of the Moslem capture of Septum on the North African coast, the Empire's westernmost stronghold, and subsequent Moslem entry into Spain. Vardan was indeed in no way to blame for the loss of Septum; the outpost almost certainly fell before his accession to the throne. But the new emperor could be charged with religious "errors," and his ardent adherence to Monotheletism was to make him so hated that he would lose his throne and his eyes before he had completed the second year of his reign. Two more emperors, Anastasius Artemius and Theodosius the Reluctant, followed in rapid succession. Anastasius might have been capable had he not been so rapidly deposed, but Theodosius, who was most "reluctant" to reign at all, proved thoroughly incompetent and with great relief abdicated the throne and retired to a monastery, where he turned out to be a far better monk than he had been a sovereign. All this occurred in the six years after Justinian's death. In 717, the strategos Leo, Justinian's one-time protégé, mounted the throne as Leo III. A new epoch was about to begin for Byzantium, while the memory of Justinian II passed into the hands of history.

We have seen how history dealt with him; how the chroniclers chose to emphasize his hot temper and unforgiving nature, how at times they actually charged him with deeds he did not commit and even when narrating plain facts usually chose to interpret his motives in the worst possible light. We have seen how this portrayal of him is distorted and unfair. If Justinian was at times a violent person, guilty of rash and unwise actions, it should also be remembered that while he was still a young man he had been subjected to the extreme cruelty of *rhinokopia*. The consciousness of the terrible disfigurement that he had to bear must have been with him almost constantly as long as he lived. If this awareness increased in him the tendencies toward arbitrary behavior already in evidence in his first reign it is understandable even if regrettable.

On the other hand, those who would interpret Justinian II would do well to place more emphasis on his remarkable ability to carry on in spite of *rhinokopia*. As an exile wandering among barbarian tribes or as emperor restored in defiance of the ancient conventions of his land, Justinian II was clearly a man of indomitable spirit. That he made serious errors, particularly in his second reign, cannot be denied. Though the motives behind some of his decisions were almost certainly less base than the chroniclers suggest, such rash acts as his reprisals against the supporters of Leontios and Apsimar and his violent attacks on Ravenna and Cherson were ill considered and unwise. Still, the clues that have come down to us, when presented fully and objectively, suggest that Justinian II possessed genuine concern for the empire over which he ruled, and in sum, when his record is weighed in the balance, he emerges as a sovereign far more responsible than the sources hostile toward him have been willing to admit.

Reference
Matter

CHRONOLOGICAL OUTLINE

OF THE LIFE AND REIGNS

OF JUSTINIAN II

669   Justinian born, probably in Constantinople, son of the Emperor Constantine IV and the Empress Anastasia.

674–678   Arabs under the Caliph Muawiya besiege Constantinople.

678   Arabs give up siege; thirty-year peace signed by Constantine IV and Muawiya.

680   Constantine IV defeated by Bulgars; forced to render tribute or "subsidy." Sixth Ecumenical Council, convoked by Constantine IV, condemns Monothelite heresy.

684   Constantine IV sends locks of his sons' hair to Pope Benedict II as token of "spiritual adoption."

685   (Probably July) Constantine IV dies, aged thirty-three. Justinian II, aged sixteen, succeeds to the throne.

685 or 686 Byzantines under command of strategos Leontios initiate hostilities against Arabs in Armenia and Iberia (Georgia).

686   (Late in the year, or early 687) Justinian holds synod to reconfirm acts of Sixth Ecumenical Council.

687   (February 17) Justinian prepares *iussio* to send to the pope, reporting on this synod and incidentally containing valuable list of the themes. Later in the same year, two imperial rescripts are sent to Pope Conon, remitting taxes and conferring other benefits on papal lands.

688   Justinian, in personal command of his forces, undertakes Sklavinian campaign, concluding with his trium-

phal entry into Thessaloniki. *Halikē* granted to clergy of St. Demetrius's Church in that city.

688 or 689   Treaty negotiated between Justinian II and the Caliph Abd-al-Malik, including condominium for Armenia, Iberia, and Cyprus, and provision for Justinian to move the Mardaïtes to locations within the Empire.

689   Justinian relocates Sklavinian prisoners of war and volunteers as military colonists in Bithynia (Opsikion theme).

c.690   Justinian begins persecution of Paulician heretics.

c.691   Justinian transports Cypriots to his new colony, Nea Justinianopolis, thus violating condominium agreement with Arabs. Probable date of Byzantine coin reform: Justinian introduces Christ effigy on obverse of his coins.

691   (Late in the year or early 692) Quinisext (Trullan) Council convoked by Justinian II in Domed (Trullan) Hall of the Imperial Palace. One hundred and two canons promulgated, largely on matters of church discipline.

692   Arab-Byzantine war breaks out. Byzantines suffer heavy defeat at Battle of Sebastopolis, when many Sklavinian troops defect to Arab side. Strategos Leontios imprisoned in Constantinople.

694 or 695   Probable date of Justinian's attempt to arrest Pope Sergius I, who has refused to ratify the Tomes of the Quinisext canons.

695   Leontios released from prison, seizes throne. Justinian mutilated and banished to Cherson.

698   Carthage falls to Arabs. Defeated Byzantine forces choose new emperor, Tiberius Apsimar. Leontios deposed, mutilated, and compelled to enter monastery.

c.699   Tiberius Apsimar returns the Cypriot colonists of Nea Justinianopolis to Cyprus.

c.704   Justinian flees from Cherson to Doros, then to Khazaria. In Khazaria he marries Theodora, sister of the Khagan Ibouzeros Gliabanos.

704   (Probably autumn) Warned by his wife of Khazar plot, Justinian escapes; crossing the Black Sea with a very

few followers, he takes refuge with Tervel, Khan of the Bulgars. Theodora remains in Khazaria.

705 (Spring) Forces of Justinian and Tervel march on Constantinople. Leo (later Emperor Leo III) joins Justinian's army. Justinian is reinstated as emperor. Meanwhile in Khazaria, Justinian's son, Tiberius, has been born.

705 (Probably summer) Patriarch Kallinikos is deposed, blinded, and banished to Rome. Other reprisals undertaken against supporters of fallen emperors. Justinian chooses Abbot Cyrus as Patriarch of Constantinople. Justinian undertakes efforts to have Pope John VII ratify the Quinisext Tomes. Theodora and infant Tiberius arrive in Constantinople and are crowned by Justinian as empress and co-emperor.

706 (February) Leontios and Tiberius Apsimar executed after public ceremony in the Hippodrome.

707 Pope John VII dies, having refused to ratify the Quinisext Tomes.

708 Justinian wars with certain Bulgars (probably not Tervel) and is defeated near Anchialos. Pope Sisinnius reigns twenty days and dies; is followed by Pope Constantine. Archbishop Felix of Ravenna refuses cooperation with papacy.

c.709 Probable date of Justinian's attack on Ravenna. Probable date of fall of Tyana to Arabs.

710 Pope Constantine leaves Rome on journey to the East. Exarch John Rizocopus dies in Ravenna; Ravenna rebellion continues.

711 Pope Constantine visits Constantinople; then confers with Justinian in Nicomedia. Compromise reached on Quinisext Canons. Justinian's expeditions sent against Cherson prove unsuccessful and eventually lead to proclamation of a rival emperor, Philippikos Vardan, backed by Khazar support.

711 (Probably November 4) Justinian beheaded. His six-year-old son, Tiberius, last heir of the Heraclian dynasty, also slain. Philippikos recognized as emperor.

HISTORICAL LISTS

610–641	Heraclius of Carthage	698–705	Tiberius III Apsimar
641	Heraclius-Constantine	705–711	Justinian II (restored)
641	Heraclonas	711–713	Philippikos Vardan
641–668	Constantine III (Constans II)	713–715	Anastasius II Artemius
668–685	Constantine IV	715–717	Theodosius III
685–695	Justinian II	717–741	Leo III
695–698	Leontios		

POPES

684–685	Benedict II	705–707	John VII
685–686	John V	708	Sisinnius
686–687	Conon	708–715	Constantine
687–701	Sergius I	715–731	Gregory II
701–705	John VI		

SELECTED BIBLIOGRAPHY

Major Early Sources (in approximate chronological order)

Sacrorum Conciliorum Nova et Amplissima Collectio. Edited by Johannes Dominicus Mansi. Vol. 11. Florence, 1755. Contains the Latin text of Justinian's *iussio* of 687 and the complete text of the Quinisext Canons in original Greek and Latin translation. Cited in the notes as Mansi, *Concilia.* English translation of the Quinisext Canons is to be found in *A Select Library of the Nicene and Post Nicene Fathers,* 2d series, edited by Philip Schaff and Henry Wace, vol. 14, New York, 1900.

Liber Pontificalis. Edited by L. Duchesne. 3 vols. 1886. Reprint, Paris, 1955. Vol. 1. The anonymous Roman *Papal Book,* a very valuable chronicle of contemporary events affecting the popes. Abbé Duchesne's edition, which was first published in the nineteenth century, includes commentary along with the Latin text.

Bede the Venerable. *De Sex Huius Saeculi Aetatibus.* Edited by Theodore Mommsen. Monumenta Germaniae Historica: Auct. Antiq., vol. 13. Berlin, 1898. The famous British monk-historian Bede makes only a few mentions of Justinian in this Latin world chronicle, but his work is interesting in that it is nearly contemporaneous with Justinian's lifetime.

Parastaseis Syntomoi Chronikai. In Patrologiae Cursus Completus: Series Gracea, edited by J.-P. Migne, vol. 157. Paris, 1866. An anonymous Byzantine fragment dating from around 750, this work is particularly valuable for some otherwise unattested insights into Justinian's quest for allies in his second reign. Migne's edition contains Greek text and Latin translation.

Ghévond. *Histoire des guerres et des conquêtes des Arabes en Arménie.* Edited and translated by Garabed V. Chahnazarian. Paris, 1856. French translation of an eighth-century Armenian chronicle. Ghévond is frequently confused on facts of Byzantine history.

Nikephoros, Patriarch of Constantinople. *Opuscula Historica* or *Brevarium.* Edited by Carolus de Boor. Leipzig, 1880. Greek text of one of the two most important chronicle sources for Justinian II. Although shorter than Theophanes' work, Nikephoros's is also probably more reliable.

Theophanes the Confessor. *Chronographia*. Edited by Carolus de Boor. 2 vols. Leipzig, 1883. Reprint. Hildesheim, 1963. Vol. 1. Greek text of the most extensive chronicle source on Justinian II.

Paul the Deacon. *Historia Langobardorum*. Edited by L. Bethmann and G. Waitz. Monumenta Germaniae Historica: Scriptores Rerum Langobardicarum et Italicarum Saec. VI–IX. Hanover, 1878. An English version of the original Latin is *History of the Langobards by Paul the Deacon*, translated by William Dudley Foulke, Philadelphia, 1905. Paul derived his data from Bede and the *Liber Pontificalis* as well as from other sources no longer extant.

Agnellus of Ravenna. "De Sancto Felice." In *Liber Pontificalis Ecclesiae Ravennatis*, edited by O. Holder-Egger. Monumenta Germaniae Historica: Scriptores Rerum Langobardicarum et Italicarum Saec. VI-IX. Hanover, 1878. Agnellus's imaginative Latin work, written in the ninth century, is a chief source for Justinian's dealings with Ravenna.

Al-Balâdhuri. *The Origins of the Islamic State*. Translated by Philip K. Hitti. New York, 1916. English translation of *Kitâb Futûḥ al-Buldân*, by a ninth-century Arabic historian of Baghdad.

Constantine VII Porphyrogenitus. *De Administrando Imperio*. Greek text edited by Gy. Moravcsik and English translation by Romilly J. H. Jenkins. Washington, 1969. Revision of first edition of Budapest, 1949. There is an accompanying volume of commentary and critical notes, *Constantine Porphyrogenitus: De Administrando Imperio, Commentary*, edited by R. J. H. Jenkins, London, 1962. Constantine VII, the very learned tenth-century Byzantine emperor, preserves important material from earlier sources.

————. *De Cerimoniis Aulae Byzantinae*. Edited by J. J. Reiskius. 2 vols. Corpus Scriptorum Historiae Byzantinae, vols. 9, 10. Bonn, 1829.

Michael the Syrian. *Chronique de Michel le Syrien*. Translated by J.-B. Chabot. 3 vols. Brussels, 1963. Vol. 2. Michael, who was Jacobite Patriarch of Antioch from 1166–99, occasionally used source materials apparently unknown to Nikephoros or Theophanes.

Gregorius Abû'l Faraj. *The Chronography of Gregory Abû'l Faraj, the Son of Aaron . . . commonly known as Bar Hebraeus*. Translated from Syriac by Ernest A. Wallis Budge. 2 vols. Oxford, 1932. Vol. 1. Bar Hebraeus, a thirteenth-century Jacobite Christian, utilized earlier sources in compiling his chronicle.

Useful Modern Works

BOOKS

Alexander, Paul J. *The Patriarch Nicephorus of Constantinople*. Oxford, 1958.

Antoniadis-Bibicou, Hélène. *Études d'histoire maritime de Byzance*. Paris, 1966.

Artamonov, M. I. *Historia Khazar*. Leningrad, 1962. In Russian.

Beševliev, Veselin. *Die Protobulgarischen Inschriften*. Berlin, 1963.

Breckenridge, James D. *The Numismatic Iconography of Justinian II*. New York, 1959.

Bury, J. B. *A History of the Later Roman Empire from Arcadius to Irene*. Vol. 2. London, 1889.

Diehl, Charles. *Études sur l'administration byzantine dans l'exarchat de Ravenne*. Paris, 1888. Reprint. New York, 1959.

————. *L'Afrique byzantine*. 2 vols. Paris, 1896. Reprint (2 vols. in 1). New York, n.d.

Dunlop, D. M. *The History of the Jewish Khazars*. Princeton, 1954.

Fliche, Augustin and Victor Martin, eds. *Histoire de l'Église*. Vol. 5. Paris, 1930.

Garsoïan, Nina G. *The Paulician Heresy*. The Hague, 1967.

Grabar, André. *L'Empereur dans l'art byzantin*. Paris, 1936.

————. *L'Iconoclasme byzantin: dossier archéologique*. Paris, 1957.

Grierson, Philip. *Catalogue of the Byzantine Coins in the Dumbarton Oaks Collection and in the Whittemore Collection*. 2 vols. to date. Washington, 1966–. Vol. 2.

Hefele, Charles Joseph. *A History of the Councils of the Church from the Original Documents*. Translated by William R. Clark. Vol. 5. Edinburgh, 1896.

Hill, Sir George. *A History of Cyprus*. 3 vols. Cambridge, 1940. Vol. 1.

Hitti, Philip K. *History of the Arabs*. 3d ed. New York, 1951.

Hodgkin, Thomas. *Italy and Her Invaders*. 8 vols. Oxford, 1895. Vol. 6.

Jenkins, Romilly. *Byzantium: The Imperial Centuries*. New York, 1966.

Krumbacher, Karl. *Geschichte der byzantinischen Litteratur von Justinian bis zum Ende des Oströmischen Reiches*. 2d ed. Munich, 1897.

Mann, Horace K. *The Lives of the Popes in the Early Middle Ages*. Vol. 1, pt. 2. 2d ed. London, 1925.

Minns, Ellis H. *Scythians and Greeks*. Cambridge, 1913.

Orosz, Louis. *The London Manuscript of Nikephoros' "Brevarium."* Budapest, 1948.

Ostrogorsky, George. *History of the Byzantine State*. 2d Eng. ed. Translated by Joan Hussey. Oxford, 1968.

Vasiliev, Alexander A. *History of the Byzantine Empire*. Madison, Wis., 1952.

Wellhausen, Julius. *The Arab Kingdom and Its Fall.* Translated by Margaret Graham Weir. 1927. Reprint. Beirut, 1963.

SHORTER MONOGRAPHS AND ARTICLES

Ashburner, Walter. "The Farmer's Law." *Journal of Hellenic Studies* 30 (1910): 85–108; 32 (1912): 68–95.

Bellinger, Alfred R. "The Copper of the Second Reign of Justinian II." *American Numismatic Society Museum Notes* 12 (1966): 122–24.

_____. "The Gold Coins of Justinian II." *Archaeology* 8 (1950): 107–11.

Beševliev, Veselin. "K voprosu o nagrade, polučennoj Tervelem ot Justiniana II v 705 g" ["On the Question of the Reward Received by Tervel from Justinian II in 705"]. *Vizantiiskii Vremenik* 16 (1959): 8–13. In Russian.

Breckenridge, James D. "The 'Long Siege' of Thessalonika: Its Date and Iconography." *Byzantinische Zeitschrift* 48 (1955): 116–22.

Brooks, E. W. "The Arabs in Asia Minor (641–750) from Arabic Sources." *Journal of Hellenic Studies* 18 (1898): 182–208.

_____. "The Brothers of the Emperor Constantine IV." *English Historical Review* 30 (1915): 42–51.

Bury, J. B. "The Great Palace." *Byzantinische Zeitschrift* 21 (1912): 210–25.

Canard, Marius. "Les Aventures d'un prisonnier arabe et d'un patrice byzantin à l'époque des guerres bulgaro-byzantines." *Dumbarton Oaks Papers* 9–10 (1956): 49–72.

Cankova-Petkova, Genoveva. "Bulgarians and Byzantium during the First Decades after the Foundation of the Bulgarian State." *Byzantinoslavica* 24 (1963): 41–53.

Charanis, Peter. "Some Remarks on the Changes in Byzantium in the Seventh Century." *Vizantološkog instituta Zbornik radova* 8, no. 1 (1963): 71–76.

_____. "The Transfer of Population as a Policy in the Byzantine Empire." *Comparative Studies in Society and History* 3 (1960–61): 140–54.

Delbrück, Richard. "Carmagnola: Porträt eines byzantinischen Kaisers." *Sonderabdruck aus den römischen Mitteilungen des Kaiserlich Deutschen Archäologischen Instituts* 29 (1914): 71–89.

Diehl, Charles. "L'Empereur au nez coupé." *Revue de Paris* 30 (1923): 71–94.

_____. "L'Origine du régime des thèmes dans l'empire byzantin." In his *Études byzantines.* Paris, 1905.

Dölger, Franz. "Ist der Nomos Georgikos ein Gesetz des Kaisers Justinian II?" *Festschrift für Leopold Wenger,* 2 vols. Munich, 1944–45. Vol. 2. (Vol. 35 in Münchener Beitrage zur Papyrusforschung und antiken Rechtsgeschichte).

Gibb, Hamilton A. R. "Arab-Byzantine Relations under the Umayyad Caliphate." *Dumbarton Oaks Papers* 12 (1958): 221–33.

Görres, Franz. "Justinian II und das römische Papsttum." *Byzantinische Zeitschrift* 17 (1908): 432–54.

Grégoire, Henri. "An Armenian Dynasty on the Byzantine Throne." *Armenian Quarterly* 1 (1946): 4–21.

————. "Un édit de l'empereur Justinien II." *Byzantion* 17 (1944–45): 119–24a.

Grierson, Philip. "The Monetary Reforms of Abd-al-Malik." *Journal of the Economic and Social History of the Orient* 3 (1960): 241–64.

————. "The Tombs and Obits of the Byzantine Emperors (337–1042)." *Dumbarton Oaks Papers* 16 (1962): 3–63.

Head, Constance. "On the Date of Justinian II's Restoration." *Byzantion* 39 (1969): 104–7.

————. "Towards a Reinterpretation of the Second Reign of Justinian II." *Byzantion* 40 (1970): 14–32.

Jenkins, Romilly J. H. "Cyprus between Byzantium and Islam, A.D. 688–965." In *Studies Presented to David Moore Robinson*, edited by George E. Mylonas and Doris Raymond. 2 vols. St. Louis, 1953. 2:1006–14.

Kaegi, Walter E. "Some Reconsiderations on the Themes." *Jahrbuch der Osterreichischen Byzantinischen Gesellschaft* 16 (1967): 39–54.

Karayannopulos, Johannes. "Entstehung und Bedeutung des Nomos Georgikos." *Byzantinische Zeitschift* 51 (1958): 357–73.

Kent, J. P. C. "The Mystery of Leontius II." *Numismatic Chronicle*, 6th series 14 (1954): 217–18.

Lemerle, Paul. "Esquisse pour une histoire agraire de Byzance." *Revue historique* 219 (1958): 32–74, 254–84.

————. "Invasions et migrations dans les Balkans depuis la fin de l'époque romaine jusqu'au VIIIe siècle." *Revue historique* 211 (1954): 265–308.

Levčenko, M. V. "Venety i prasiny v Vizantii v V-VII vv." ["Blues and Greens in Byzantium in the Fifth to Seventh Centuries"]. *Vizantiiskii Vremenik* 1 (1947): 164–83. In Russian.

Maricq, André. "La Durée du régime des partis populaires à Constantinople." *Bulletin de la Classe des Lettres et des Sciences Morales et Politiques.* 5th ser. 35 (Brussels, 1949): 63–74.

————. "Notes sur les Slaves dans le Péloponnèse et en Bithynie et sur l'emploi de 'Slave' comme appelatif." *Byzantion* 22 (1952): 337–55.

Ostrogorsky, George. "The Byzantine Empire in the World of the Seventh Century." *Dumbarton Oaks Papers* 13 (1959): 1–21.

————. "Byzantium and the South Slavs." *The Slavonic and East European Review* 42 (1963–64): 1–14.

————. "Das Steuersystem im byzantinischen Altertum und Mittelalter." *Byzantion* 6 (1931): 229–40.

Setton, Kenneth M. "On the Importance of Land Tenure and Agrarian Taxation in the Byzantine Empire." *American Journal of Philology* 74 (1953): 225–59.

Stein, Ernst. "Vom Altertum im Mittelalter zur Geschichte der byzantinischen Finanzverwaltung." *Vierteljahrschrift für Sozial- und Wirtschaftsgeschichte* 21 (1928): 158–70.

Vasiliev, Alexander A. "An Edict of the Emperor Justinian II." *Speculum* 18 (1943): 1–13.

————. "L'Entrée triomphale de l'empereur Justinien II à Thessalonique en 688." *Orientalia Christiana Periodica* 13 (1947): 356–68.

————. "The Historical Significance of the Mosaic of Saint Demetrius at Sassoferrato." *Dumbarton Oaks Papers* 5 (1950): 31–39.

Vernadskij, Georges. "Sur les origines de la Loi agraire byzantine." *Byzantion* 2 (1925): 169–80.

INDEX